WITHDRAWN

FOR REFERENCE

NOT TO BE TAKEN FROM THE ROOM

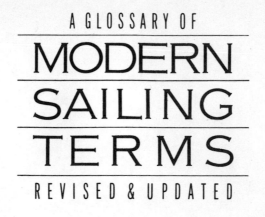

A GLOSSARY OF

MODERN
SAILING
TERMS

REVISED & UPDATED

A GLOSSARY OF

MODERN

SAILING

TERMS

REVISED & UPDATED

John Rousmaniere

G.P. Putnam's Sons • New York

G. P. Putnam's Sons
Publishers Since 1838
200 Madison Avenue
New York, NY 10016

Library of Congress Cataloging-in-Publication Data
Rousmaniere, John.
    A glossary of modern sailing terms /
    John Rousmaniere. — 2nd ed.

        p.   cm.
1. Sailing—Dictionaries.   I. Title.
    GV811.R59 1989   87-36603 CIP
    797.1'24'03—dcl9

ISBN 0-399-15005-6
Printed in the United States of America
1   2   3   4   5   6   7   8   9   10

Once again for my parents.

Preface

Propelled by the wind of technology, the sailor's vocabulary races on into new waters. Thus the requirement for a revised edition of this small book, originally written in 1973. Back then, my purpose was to provide a handy guide to the fundamental terms in the language of modern sailors. The book met a need both among novices intimidated by such mind-benders as the multiple meanings of the words *lay* and *run* and among experienced sailors baffled by terms like *360 rule* and *decksweeper* that had made their way from the decks of racing boats into the pages of the yachting magazines.

I hope that this new edition will be equally helpful. Of the approximately twelve hundred terms in the original, I have rewritten or replaced more than four hundred. My guide throughout has been proper contemporary usage. I began this revision by carefully reading several national boating magazines published in the spring of 1987, noting not only those terms that might confuse a new sailor but also the absence of terms that were fairly common back in 1973. In adding new terms and dropping old ones, I have had to cut a few dear friends that, these days, rarely appear except in memory.

The reader should be aware that very many terms in the sailor's vocabulary can serve as verbs as well as nouns. For example, a sailor *reefs* a sail by tying in a *reef*, and a boat *tacks* onto starboard *tack*. To save space, I have not made a special point of indicating that a word can be used as more than one part of speech except to give examples of complicated usage.

This is a brief guide to popular usage and *not* a detailed, academic dictionary of all technical and traditional boating terms. Anybody looking for more specialized and encyclopedic coverage will want to consult an instructional manual on navigation, boatbuilding, and other skills. I also recommend a look at the following dictionaries: René de Kerchove's huge *International Maritime Dictionary* (1961), Gershom Bradford's meticulous *The Mariner's Dictionary* (1972), and John V. Noel's thorough *The Boating Dictionary* (1980).

The idea for this book was not mine but rather that of the late Critchell Rimington, the former publisher and editor of *Yachting* magazine and a marvelous man who is greatly missed by those who knew him. He very generously put me in touch with a book publisher and warmly provided encouragement when I needed it. Every writer working on his or her first book should have such a sponsor.

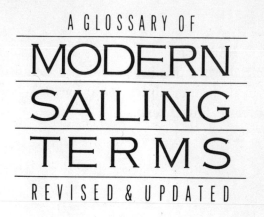

A GLOSSARY OF

MODERN

SAILING

TERMS

REVISED & UPDATED

NOTE TO READERS

An italicized word or phrase within a definition is defined in its proper alphabetical location, as are many other technical terms.

A

Aback. See *Back*.

Abaft. Behind, aft of. "Abaft the beam" is the area between dead abeam and dead astern.

Abeam. At right angles to a boat's centerline. Also, "on the beam."

Able. Seaworthy and fast.

Aboard. In a boat.

Accommodation Plan. See *Plan*.

Accommodations. Living areas and furniture in a boat, including *bunks*, *heads*, and a *galley*.

Acockbill. See *Cockbilled*.

Admiral's Cup. Awarded to the national team that wins a biennial series of ocean races off England.

Adrift. Drifting, unsecured.

Aerodynamics. The principles of the flow of air around objects.

Afloat. Floating.

Aft. Toward the stern. Illustration on page 3.

After. Denotes location toward the boat's stern, e. g., "afterbody" (the back portion of the *hull* beneath the water), "after cabin" (a *cabin* on the stern), "after-deck" (the deck near the stern), and "after guy" (the *guy* that leads *aft*).

After Cabin Layout.   See *Midships Cockpit Layout.*

Afterguard.   Originally a ship's officers, but now those with greatest responsibility in a racing boat's crew: the owner, navigator, and watch captains.

Aground.   Describes a boat whose hull or keel is stuck on the bottom in shallow water. "To run aground" is to become so stuck.

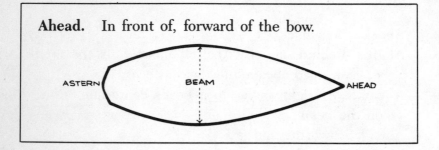

Ahead.   In front of, forward of the bow.

ASTERN   BEAM   AHEAD

A-Hull.   Riding out a storm with no sails up. Also, "lying a-hull."

Aid to Navigation.   A *buoy, daybeacon,* or *lighthouse* established and maintained by a government agency or private organization (for example, a *yacht club*) to indicate a channel. See *Buoy, Cardinal System, Lateral System.*

Air.   Wind, breeze.

Air Tank.   A watertight compartment built into a boat or an inflated rubber tube secured in the boat. Both help to keep the boat from sinking if she fills with water (fiberglass does not float).

Alee.   Away from the wind, to leeward. A helmsman cries "hard alee" or "helm's alee" as he pushes the tiller to leeward to tack.

All Hands.   The entire crew.

Aloft. Above the deck, generally in the rigging. Illustration on page 109.

Alongshore. Near shore. Opposite of *offshore*. Also, "longshore."

Alongside. Beside another boat or a pier.

Alter Course. To change the direction in which a boat is sailing or motoring.

Alternative Penalty. A penalty other than disqualification for a foul during a race. Penalties include sailing one or two complete circles (see *360/720 Rule*) and a change to a lower finish position.

American Bureau of Shipping (ABS). An organization of naval architects that has compiled *scantlings* for ships, boats, and yachts.

America's Cup. A trophy awarded to the winner of an international best-of-seven-race *match race* series sailed in sailing yachts. The trophy is named for the U.S. yacht *America*, which won it in England in 1851. U.S. yachts won every match until 1983, when an Australian yacht won it. A U.S. yacht rewon the trophy in 1987.

Amidship(s). Toward the middle of the boat, equidistant between bow and stern. Also, "midship(s)."

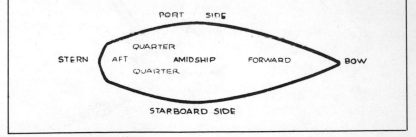

Anchor.   A steel or aluminum device at the end of a line or chain (*anchor rode*). The anchor "flukes" dig into the bottom and the rode keeps the boat attached. Anchors are available in various combinations of shape, size, and weight. Some combinations hold better in certain bottoms than others. When an anchor holds, it "bites"; when it does not, it "drags." Also called "hook."

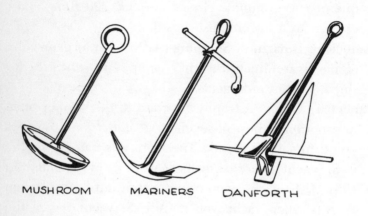

MUSHROOM   MARINERS   DANFORTH

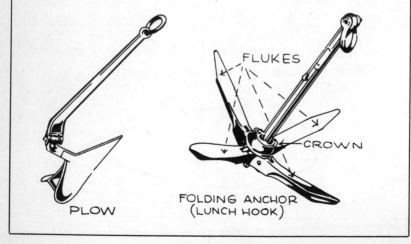

FLUKES

CROWN

PLOW

FOLDING ANCHOR
(LUNCH HOOK)

Anchor Rode. The *line*, chain, or combination of the two that connects the anchor and the boat. See *Anchor, Scope*.

Anchor Watch. See *Watch*.

Anchor Well. A *locker* recessed in the foredeck for stowing the *anchor*.

Anemometer. A device that measures the wind's speed and shows it on an indicator.

Angle of Attack. The angle between the sail and the wind or the *hull, keel,* or *rudder* and the boat's *course*.

Anti-Fouling Paint. Paint applied to a boat's underbody to prevent growth of barnacles or weed.

Apparent Wind. The strength and direction of the wind that is felt in a moving boat: compare with *True Wind*.

Apparent Wind Indicator. A device that shows the direction of the *apparent wind*.

Appendage. A fin projecting into the water from the hull: *centerboard, keel, rudder,* or *skeg*.

Aspect Ratio. The numerical ratio between a sail's, rig's, rudder's, centerboard's, or keel's height (or depth) and its width. A relatively narrow sail, etc., has a "high aspect ratio." A relatively wide one has a "low aspect ratio."

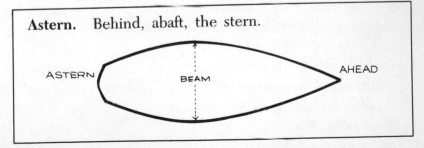

Astern. Behind, abaft, the stern.

ASTERN   BEAM   AHEAD

Athwartships. Across the boat, either inboard (toward the centerline) or outboard (toward the gunwale).

Automatic Pilot. An electronic device that steers a boat on a desired *compass course*, without need for a *steerer.* Compare with *Self-Steerer.*

Auxiliary. 1) An engine that provides motive power in a sailboat or electrical power in any boat. 2) Abbreviation for "auxiliary sailboat" or a sailboat with an auxiliary engine.

Awash. When seas wash over a boat's decks or over a reef.

Aweigh. Describes an anchor that is off the bottom and being hoisted.

Awning. A canvas or synthetic cloth hung over the cockpit to provide shade.

B

Babystay. See *Stay.*

Back. 1) To trim a sail to the windward side. A sail so trimmed is "backed" or "aback." A boat is "caught aback" when the sails are suddenly backed by a drastic wind *shift.* 2) To shift in a counterclockwise direction, for example "the wind backed from North to Northwest." Opposite of *veer.*

Back Eddy. Water motion opposite to the general current flow, caused by the current reflecting off piers, islands, or points of land.

Back Off. See *Pawl.*

Backstay. See *Stay.*

Backstay Adjustor. See *Stay Adjustor.*

Backwind. Air flowing aft off the leech of the jib into the leeward side of the mainsail, or off the sails of one close-hauled boat into those of another off her windward quarter.

Baggy Wrinkle. A bushy winding of rope yarns that is secured to a spreader or stay to help prevent chafe on sails. See *Chafe.*

Bail. To remove water with a bucket.

Bailers. Small retractable sluices in the bilge of a small boat through which bilge water passes when the boat is moving rapidly.

Balance. The degree to which the various forces on a sailboat balance out each other. If the forces are "unbalanced," the boat is hard to steer. A "well balanced" boat sails easily with slight *weather helm,* while a "poorly balanced" boat has considerable weather or lee helm.

Bale. A curved metal strap.

Ballast. Weight in a boat below the *waterline,* either in the *bilge* ("internal ballast") or in the *keel* ("external ballast"), that helps provide *stability.*

Ballast-Displacement Ratio. The ratio between the weight of a boat's ballast and her total displacement, expressed as a percentage.

Bank. A large navigable shoal-water area.

Bar. An area of shoal water at the entrance to a river or harbor.

Barber Hauler. A line used to adjust the *athwartships* position of the jib *sheet.*

Bareboat Charter. A charter of a cruising boat that has no paid hands. Frequently abbreviated to "bareboat."

Barging. Forcing maneuvering room to windward of another boat at the start of a race. It is not illegal to barge, but barging can lead to violation of the basic racing rule of "windward boat keep clear."

Barney Post. A post in the *cockpit* to which the main *sheet* is led.

Barometer. An instrument that indicates atmospheric pressure in inches or *millibars*. A "barograph" records the readings on graph paper. Also, "glass."

Batten. A thin, narrow slat made of wood, fiberglass, or some other strong, flexible material that is inserted into a pocket in the *leech* of a *mainsail*, *mizzen*, or small *jib* to help keep the leech from fluttering. A "full-length batten" runs the width of the sail.

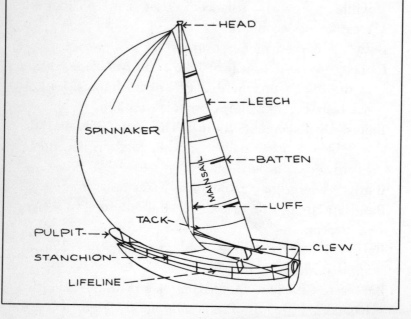

Batten Down. Originally, to secure hatch covers tightly. Now, to prepare a boat for rough weather.

BC. Abbreviation for "boat club" or "beach club."

Beach Boat. A boat small and light enough to be easily pulled up on a beach.

Beacon. See *Daybeacon*.

Beam. The width of a boat on *deck*. The "maximum beam" (Bm.) is listed in dimensions. A "beamy boat" has relatively wide beam for her length; a "narrow boat" has narrow beam. "On her beam's end" describes a boat that is *heeled* very far over.

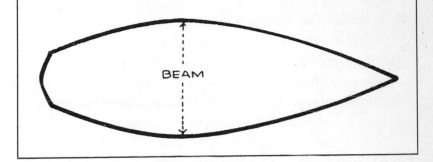

BEAM

Bear Away. See *Head Off*.

Bearing. The direction between the boat and another object. A "relative bearing" is the inscribed angle between the boat's *bow* and the object. A "compass bearing" is the direction in *magnetic* degrees as shown on the *compass*. See *Compass, Pelorus*.

Bear Off. See *Head Off*.

Beat. Upwind leg of a race. A "dead beat" is a leg directly into the wind. "To beat" is to sail *close-hauled*.

Beaufort Scale. A wind scale invented by the English Admiral Sir Francis Beaufort in the early-nineteenth century. Wind and sea conditions are related in thirteen Forces—from Force O, Calm, to Force 12, Hurricane. In the middle, Force 6 is a Strong Breeze of 22-27 knots that produces (at sea) nine-foot waves with extensive foam crests. A gale is Force 8, with 34-40 knots of wind and eighteen-foot waves.

Before the Wind. See *Off Wind*.

Bell Buoy. See *Buoy, Lateral System*.

Bells. See *Ship's Clock*.

Below. Beneath decks; in a cabin.

Bend. Turns in a *line* to *secure* it to another line or a *spar*. See *Hitch, Knot*.

Bend On. To install a piece of *gear*, for example "bend on the *jib*" "bend on the *anchor rode*."

Bendy Rig. A mast that can be easily bent *aft* in order to change the shape of the *mainsail*.

Bermuda Race. A race to Bermuda held in even-numbered years from Newport, Rhode Island, and in odd-numbered years from Marion, Massachusetts.

Bermudian Rig. See *Marconi Rig*.

Berth. 1) For a person, a bed in a boat. 2) For a boat, a mooring location at a pier. 3) A "wide berth" is a margin of safety. 4) A "crew's berth" is a position in a crew.

Bias Strain. Tension in a sail that runs parallel neither to the warp fibers that run the length of a panel of sailcloth nor to the woof (fill) fibers that run the panel's width. Bias strains will stretch the cloth to an extreme and frequently unpredictable degree, and thus change the sail's shape.

Bight. 1) Any part of a line between the ends. 2) A shallow cove.

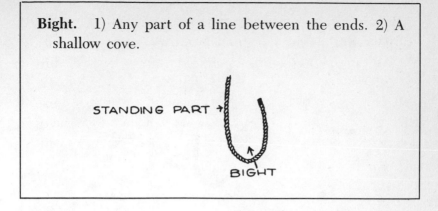

STANDING PART →

BIGHT

Bilge. 1) The lowest part of the hull below the waterline generally below the sole or floorboards. Water collects there in the sump. 2) The curve from the topsides to the boat's bottom, sometimes called "the turn of the bilge." With a "hard" or "sharp bilge," the curve is abrupt; with a "soft" or "easy bilge," it is gradual.

Bilge Pump. A pump for exhausting water overboard from the bilge. Its intake is usually in the sump.

Bilge Tank. A water or fuel tank installed under the floorboards in the bilge.

Bin. Recessed stowage compartment for sails, lines, or other equipment.

Binnacle. In a cockpit, a pedestal on top of which a compass is secured. Generally the steering wheel is on the after side of the binnacle. A "binnacle compass" is a compass in a binnacle.

Bite. See *Anchor.*

Bitt. A post for securing *docking* and *mooring lines.* A small bitt on the deck of a sailboat is called a "samson post."

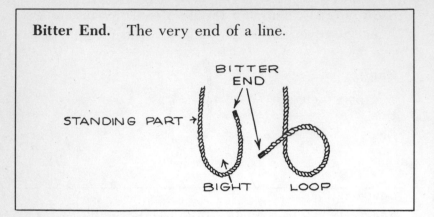
Black Flag. A signal flown by a race committee to indicate that a boat is disqualified for starting the race prematurely.

Blanket. To prevent the wind from reaching another boat's sails by sailing directly *upwind* of her.

Blind Man's Test. A technique used to examine a wire for frayed strands by rubbing it with a hand or a rag.

Block. A pulley on a boat. A roller called a *sheave* is hung between two supports called "cheeks" either on a pin ("sheave pin") or on ball-bearing races. There are many types of blocks. A "snatch block" opens to receive *line*. A "fixed block" remains closed. A "single block" has one sheave, a "double block" two sheaves, and so on. A "becket block" has a fixed *eye* as well as one or more sheaves. A "bullet block" is very small. A "cheek block" is open on one side. A "turning block" redirects a line. A "foot block" lies flat on *deck*.

Block and Tackle. See *Tackle*.

Blooper. A lightweight, full overlapping jib set on ocean racers when running.

Blue Water. As a noun, deep water or the ocean. As an adjective, describes a sailor or boat with ocean sailing experience.

Bluff-Bowed. Describes a boat with wide, full bow sections. Also, *full-ended.*

Bm. Abbreviation for "extreme beam." See *Beam.*

Board. 1) To go on a boat, to go aboard. 2) A leg or tack when sailing close-hauled. 3) Abbreviation for *"centerboard."*

Boarding Gate. See *Gangway.*

Boardsailing. See *Sailboard.*

Boat. Any vessel smaller than a ship or, traditionally, any vessel small enough to be carried in a ship. A boat may be used for pleasure or for business. All yachts are boats; so are some smaller Navy and Coast Guard vessels. Boat is not a verb.

Boat Club. Yacht club.

Boater. Traditionally, a straw hat, but now used to describe a person who uses a boat. See *Yachtsman, Yachtswoman.*

Boat Hook. A pole with a hook in the end, used to grab line.

Boating. Pertaining to boats.

Boat Speed. A boat's speed through the water in knots or miles per hour. See *Speed Made Good, Speedometer.*

Boatswain. Pronounced "bo'sun." The crewmember assigned to maintenance of gear. "Boatswain's work" includes splicing and whipping line and wire rope, cleaning and maintaining all running and standing rigging. A "boatswain's chair" is a short board or a sling suspended by a bridle from a halyard on which a crewmember is hauled aloft to inspect rigging.

BOAT/U.S. The Boat Owners Association of the United States, a lobbying organization and equipment supplier.

Boat Yard. A commercial operation where boats are built, painted, stored, and repaired.

Bobstay. A stay or chain running from the end of a bowsprit to the stem to help support the sprit. It may run over a strut extending downward from the bowsprit called a dolphin striker.

BOC Race. A quadrennial around-the-world race for singlehanded boats.

Body. The shape of a boat's *hull*. Originally "body plan." See *Underbody*.

Body of Water. An area of *navigable* water, for example a bay, lake, or harbor.

Bold. Steep.

Bollards. On a pier or boat, two vertical posts, or heads, of wood or iron to which mooring lines are attached.

Bolt Rope. Rope secured to the edge of a sail to give it strength and to facilitate adjusting foot and luff tension.

Bomb. A meteorological term describing a storm in which the barometer reading drops extremely rapidly, at a rate of 1 millibar (0.03 inch) an hour or more for a 24-hour period.

Boom. A *spar* that holds out a sail's clew. See also *Wishbone Boom*.

Boom Crotch. A temporary support for a boom when the sail is not hoisted.

Boom Jack. See *Vang*.

Boomkin. A short strut extending aft from the transom to support the mizzen sheet blocks or the backstay.

Boom Vang.   See *Vang.*

Boot Top.   A painted band running the full length of the hull just above and parallel to the waterline.

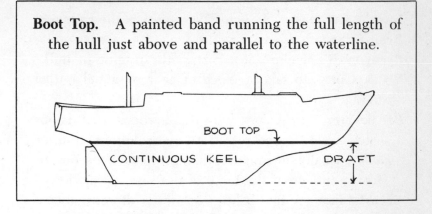

Bottom.   1) The land covered by water. 2) The lowest part of a boat's hull underwater.

Bow.   The front of the boat. The "bow wave" is the wave near the bow that is created by the bow pushing through the water.

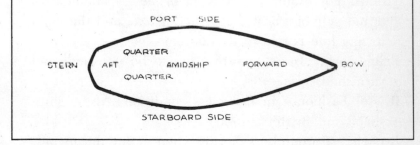

Bowditch.   Shorthand for Nathaniel Bowditch's *American Practical Navigator,* U.S. Hydrographic Office publication No. 9.

Bow Roller.   A rubber wheel on the *stem* or a *bow-*

sprit over which the *anchor rode* is led. Also, "stem roller."

Bowsprit.   A rod or plank extending forward from the *stem* to support the *bow roller* or the jib *tack.*

Box the Compass.   To name the points of the compass.

Braid.   See *Rope.*

Breakdown.   Failure of a part in the rigging or hull.

Break Out.   To take a piece of gear or a sail out of stowage.

Breakwater.   1) A low bulwark on deck that keeps water out of the cockpit. 2) An embankment, spur, or *mole,* usually manmade, that protects a harbor or river mouth from the force of the seas. Also, "jetty."

Breast Line.   A tie-up line that leads directly abeam from a boat to a pier or float.

Breeze.   Wind, air.

Bridge.   See *Flying Bridge.*

Bridge Deck.   A narrow *deck* separating the *cockpit* from the companionway.

Bridle.   A line secured to the same object at both ends. For example a "towing bridle" is attached to either side of a boat that is under *tow,* and the main towing line is tied to its middle.

Brightwork.   Brass gear that has to be polished, and varnished surfaces.

Bristol Fashion.   In first-class condition. Also, "ship-shape and Bristol fashion."

Broach.   To round up sharply when sailing downwind, but frequently used to connote loss of steering control. Also, "broach to."

Broad Off the Bow (Quarter).   Describes an object

bearing about 45 degrees from the bow (or stern). Also, "broad on. . . ."

Broken Water. Water with irregular or steep waves.

Broker. In the context of boating, someone who sells and rents boats.

Brummel Hook. A slotted aluminum or bronze eye. One hook links into another when slots are matched.

Bubble Sextant. A sextant with a bubble that serves as an artificial horizon when the natural horizon is unclear. See *Sextant*.

Built-In. Describes an object that is secured to the hull, e.g., "built-in berth."

Bulkhead. An athwartship-running wall that separates cabins and usually is integral to the hull's construction.

Bulwark. A plank or series of planks on edge a foot or more high extending around the perimeter of the deck on the rail, to keep out water in rough weather.

Bunkboard. A wooden slat or Dacron sheet that keeps a sleeping crew member from falling out of a windward berth when the boat heels.

Buoy. An anchored, floating object used as a part of a mooring, a mark in a race course, or an aid to navigation to indicate a channel. When used as aids to navigation, buoys have distinctive shapes, colors, numbers, and light characteristics, and are arranged in patterns called "buoyage." In the lateral system of buoyage used almost everywhere in the United States, there are several types of buoys. A "nun" is red, even numbered, and conical at the top. A "can" is green or black, odd-numbered, and flat at the top. There are three types of "sound buoy": a "whistle" makes a low moan, a "bell" has a single-toned bell, and a "gong" has a multi-toned bell. "Lighted buoys" (which may also have sounds) have white, red, or green lights whose patterns are called "light phase characteristics." Other buoys used as aids to navigation indicate the centers and intersections of channels, anchorages, danger areas, etc. Buoys are also used as aids to navigation in the *cardinal system*, where their distinctive colors and shapes indicate the location of shoals.

Buoyancy. The upward-pushing force that keeps an object afloat.

Burdened Vessel. See *Give-Way Vessel*.

Burgee. A small flag, usually swallowtailed, with a boatowner's or a yacht club's signal.

Buttocks. 1) A boat's after underbody. 2) Buttock lines on a plan show fore and aft sections taken at various distances from the centerline and indicate the relative fullness of the bow and stern.

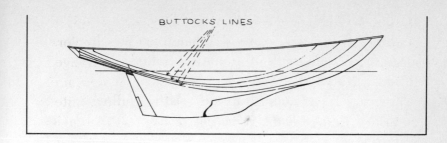

BUTTOCKS LINES

By the Lee. Sailing on a run with the wind coming over the quarter on which the boom is trimmed instead of dead over the stern or over the windward quarter. There is a danger that the wind will catch behind the mainsail and precipitate an accidental jibe.

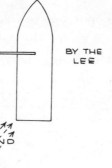

BY THE
LEE

WIND

C

Cabin. A room in a boat.

Cabin Lights. Kerosene or electric lights that illuminate a boat's cabin.

Cabin Trunk. See *Trunk*.

Cable. 1) A heavy rope or chain. 2) Two hundred yards, or one-tenth of a nautical mile.

Calm. No wind.

Camber. 1) A sail's draft or relative fullness. See *Chord, Flat, Full, Depower, Power.* 2) A deck's crown.

Can Buoy. See *Buoy, Lateral System.*

Canoe Stern. See *Double-Ender.*

Canvas. Sails.

Capsize. To turn over.

Capstan. An electric- or muscle-driven winch on the foredeck used to pull heavy loads, such as the anchor rode.

Captain. 1) The person in charge of a commercial vessel. 2) In a yacht, the chief of the paid hands, if any; the amateur in charge of a yacht is the *skipper.*

Car. An adjustable slide or block that runs on a track. Cars are used on deck for the jib sheet, on the mast for the inboard end of the spinnaker pole, and on the traveler for the main sheet.

Cardinal System. A buoyage system of indicating channels in which the distinctive shape and color of a buoy shows the direction to nearby hazards to navigation. Compare with *Lateral System.*

Cardinal Points of a Compass. North, South, East, and West. Northeast, Southeast, Southwest, and Northwest are called "intercardinal points." See *-ing*.

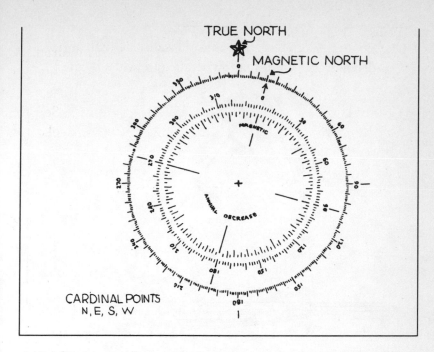

TRUE NORTH

MAGNETIC NORTH

MAGNETIC

ANNUAL DECREASE

CARDINAL POINTS
N, E, S, W

Carline. A fore-and-aft-running beam under the deck, usually around a hatch opening.

Carry Away. To break or to be washed overboard.

Carvel-Planked. Wooden boat construction in which the topside planks are butted against each other. Opposite of *lapstrake construction.*

Cast Off. To let go a line.

Catamaran. A multihulled boat with two narrow hulls linked by a deck or by crossbeams. Its great speed is derived from the stability afforded by its beam. Abbreviated "cat."

Cat Rig. A *sail plan* with a *mainsail* but no *jib.* A "cat ketch" or "cat yawl" carries two cat-rigged *masts,* the *after* one shorter than the *forward* one.

Cat Boat. A one- or two-masted sailboat with no jib and generally with shallow draft and wide beam.

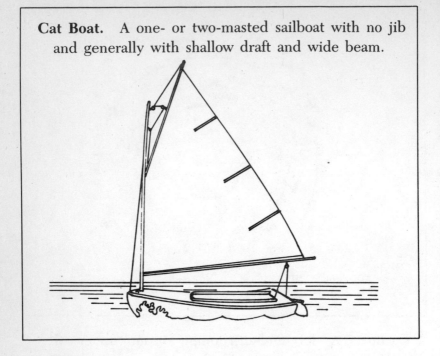

Cat's Paw. A light puff of wind. It makes a paw-shaped pattern on the water.

Caught Aback. See *Back*.

Cavitation. The revolution of a propeller in the air or in broken water, producing little if any drive force.

CCA. The Cruising Club of America.

Celestial Navigation. The branch of *navigation* that uses the sun, moon, stars, planets, a *sextant*, and astronomical tables. Compare with *Dead Reckoning, Piloting*.

Centerboard. Frequently, "board." A retractable metal, wooden, or fiberglass slab that hangs off a pin ("centerboard pin") in a cavity ("centerboard trunk") from the boat's bottom or keel. A "centerboarder" is a boat with a centerboard.

Center Cockpit Layout. See *Midships Cockpit Layout*.

Centerline. The imaginary straight line that runs fore and aft along the exact center of the boat.

Center of Effort (CE). The center of pressure of the wind on the *sail plan*.

Center of Gravity (CG). The place in the boat where all the weights balance each other out.

Center of Lateral Resistance (CLR). The center of pressure of the water on the *underbody*.

Chafe. Wear on running rigging or on sails. Chafing gear (hoses, leather, cloth, *baggy wrinkle*) is used to prevent chafe by one object on another.

Chain. See *Anchor Rode*.

Chain Hook. A metal claw that grabs and secures chain.

Chain Locker. A *locker* in the bow where the *anchor rode* is stowed when the boat is *underway*. Sometimes the *forepeak*.

Chain Plates. Sturdy bronze or stainless-steel straps bolted into the hull; stays are secured to them.

Chance. Heavy weather. Sometimes, "hard chance."

Channel. Water deep enough for most boats to sail in. See *Lateral System*.

Chanty. Sometimes, "chantey." Sung by professional seamen on commercial sailing vessels to give rhythm and pace to their work. Pronounced, and sometimes spelled, "shanty." The "chantyman" led the songs.

Chapman's. Short for a boating manual titled *Piloting, Seamanship, and Small Boat Handling*, originally written in 1922 by Charles F. Chapman.

Character Boat. An older, traditional design, such as a Friendship sloop.

Characteristics. The color and pattern of lights on lighthouses and lighted buoys. A light's "phase characteristic" is its sequence and timing.

Chart. A map of a *body of water* and (usually) the adjoining land. The "chart scale" is a number indicating the size of the area covered and the amount of detail. "Large-scale charts" (for example, with a scale of 1 inch : 50,000 inches) cover small areas in great detail, while "small-scale charts" (1 : 1,000,000 or more) cover large areas in limited detail. See illustration on page 25. The "chart table" is a table below on which the *navigator* works on charts. "To chart" a course, bearing, or position is to draw it on a chart.

Charter. To rent a boat.

Cheater. Slang for "spinnaker staysail." See *Staysail*.

Cheeks. The sides of a block. See *Block*.

Chine. In a V-bottom boat, the angle of intersection between topsides and bottom. It is improper to term a round-bottomed boat a "soft-chine vessel," for a round-bilged boat has no chine at all.

Chock. A metal groove or slot on the *bow*, *stern*, or *rail* through which the *anchor rode*, *docking lines*, and *mooring lines* are *led*, or passed onto the boat.

Chock-a-Block. Two-blocked. See *Block*.

Chop. Sea condition with frequent steep waves, usually the result of wind and current running in opposite directions.

Chord. An imaginary line drawn across a sail from *luff* to *leech* that is used to provide mathematical descriptions of the sail's shape. To calculate the *camber* (*draft*) of a sail, measure the "chord length," then divide that length into the "chord depth," or the

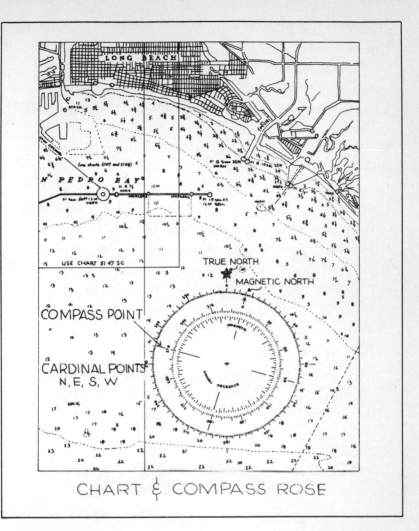

LONG BEACH

N PEDRO BAY

USE CHART 5147 SC

TRUE NORTH

MAGNETIC NORTH

COMPASS POINT

CARDINAL POINTS
N, E, S, W

CHART & COMPASS ROSE

distance between the chord and the sail at its deepest. The resulting ratio is the sail's camber. To calculate the "draft position," measure how far back the deepest point is and divide it by the chord length. The two ratios that result may be compared with those of other sails. See *Flat, Full, Depower, Power.*

Chowder. A thick fish soup.

Chronometer. An extremely accurate timepiece, usually factory-calibrated and guaranteed to retain accuracy longer than ordinary clocks or watches.

Chute. Slang for *spinnaker*. Derived from "parachute."

Circumnavigate. To sail around something, usually the world.

Clam Cleat. See *Cleat*.

Class. A group of boats similar in size or type that start a race together and have their own prizes.

Claw Off. To sail upwind away from a lee shore.

Clear. Free of or to be freed from restrictions, such as "clear air" (wind not affected by boats or obstructions) or "to clear customs."

Cleat. A device for securing ("cleating") *lines*. The line is wrapped several times around a "horn cleat," wrapped once around a "jam cleat," and laid between the jaws of a "cam cleat" or "Clam Cleat."

CLEAT   JAM CLEAT

CAM CLEAT   CLAM CLEAT

Clevis Pin. A bronze or stainless steel pin that fits into and secures one fitting to another. It may be threaded or it may have a small hole into which a *cotter pin* is slipped to keep the clevis pin in the fitting. Illustration on page 124.

Clew. The after lower corner of a jib, mainsail, or mizzen and one of the two lower corners of a spinnaker. Illustration on page 8.

Clinker-Planked. See *Lapstrake Construction.*

Clinometer. An instrument indicating angle of heel.

Clipper Bow. A bow whose stem profile is concave.

Close. To approach.

Close Aboard. Near.

Closed Course. A race course around buoys rather than between two points.

Close-Hauled. Sailing as close to the wind as possible. Also, "on the wind."

Close-Winded. Describes a boat able to sail especially close to the wind when close-hauled.

Club-Footed Jib. A jib with a boom.

CMG. See *Course Made Good*.

Coaming. A low rail around a *cockpit*.

Coastal Navigation. See *Piloting*.

Coast Guard. The United States Coast Guard (USCG), the military agency charged with supervising the nation's boating areas. Its volunteer arm, the United States Coast Guard Auxiliary (USCGA), provides courtesy inspections of safety equipment for pleasure boats and teaches boating skills in its many flotillas.

Coast Pilot. A U.S. government publication providing detailed descriptions of and advice about boating areas and harbors.

Cockbilled. Describes an anchor hanging over the bow and ready to be dropped. Also, "acockbill."

Cockpit. A recessed area in the deck for the crew.

Cockpit Awning. See *Awning*.

Cockpit Cover. A canvas or synthetic fabric sheet stretched over a cockpit to keep dirt and water out when the boat is not in use.

Code Flag. A flag representing, in the International Code, a number, letter, or phrase.

Coffee Grinder. A large, powerful winch driven by handles.

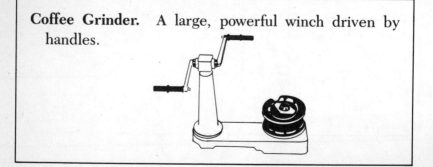

Coil. To arrange a line in loops to be hung from a cleat, winch, or other object so the line does not tangle or kink.

Colors. 1) The ensign, or national flag. 2) The time of day when the ensign is raised or lowered.

COLREGS. See *Rules of the Road*.

Come About. See *Tack*, Def. No. 2.

Come Up. See *Head Up*.

Commission. To prepare a boat for a sailing season. A boat "in commission" is prepared, launched, and ready for use.

Committee Boat. Vessel used by the race committee to start and finish races.

Commodore. A yacht club's highest officer.

Companionway. A passageway from the *deck* or *cockpit* to the *cabin* below via a ladder. It may be shut off in *heavy weather* with wooden boards or Plexiglas slats, sometimes called wash boards.

Compass. The device that indicates *magnetic direction*. It consists of a magnetized card ("compass card") floating in light oil (which dampens its swing) inside a glass dome (which magnifies the card for the viewer). The card orients itself toward magnetic North. It is marked with the four *cardinal points* and the 360 degrees between them. Posts called "lubber's lines" facilitate "steering by the compass" and "taking a bearing." The "steering compass" is permanently mounted in the *cockpit* where the *steerer* can easily see it. A "hand-bearing compass" is a hand-held compass designed especially for taking bearings. A "telltale compass" is a compass located *below* where other members of the crew can keep track of courses steered. See *Compass Direction*.

Compass Adjuster.   A technician who corrects errors in compasses. See *Compass Error, Deviation*.

Compass Direction.   Headings, courses, and bearings as read on the compass, as against magnetic and true directions as read on a chart's compass rose.

Compass Error.   The difference in degrees between headings and bearings as read on the boat's compass and the same headings and bearings in true degrees due to the sum effect of deviation and variation.

Compass Point.   One of thirty-two directions on a compass, at 11¼ degree intervals. Illustration on page 21.

Compass Rose.   A circle on a chart similar to that in a compass. It orients the chart to true North and magnetic North. Illustration on page 25.

Continuous Keel.   See *Keel*.

Cored Construction.   See *Fiberglass Construction*.

Corinthian.   An amateur sailor.

Corrected Time.   See *First*.

Cotter Pin.   A small bronze or stainless steel wire ring or pin used to secure the *clevis pins* in a block or a shackle or to keep *turnbuckles* from rotating.

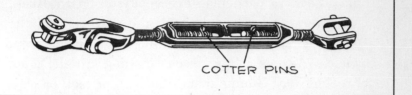

COTTER PINS

Course.   1) The direction in which the boat is sailing (sometimes "heading") as gauged either by nearby objects or by the *compass* ("compass course"; see *Compass Direction*). To "alter course" is to change direction. To "hold course" is to stay sailing in one direction. To sail "off course" is to wander from the desired course. To sail "on course" is to steer the desired course. The "proper course" is the course that keeps the boat out of danger. 2) The sequence of *marks* in a race.

Course Made Good (CMG).   The course that the boat effectively sails taking into account her compass course, the steerer's errors, current, waves, leeway, and other factors that push or pull her to one side or the other. Also, "course over the bottom." See *Speed Made Good*.

Courtesy Flag.   The flag of the host nation flown in the *starboard rigging* of a visiting *vessel*.

Cove.   A small harbor.

Cove Stripe.   A decorative stripe running fore and aft on the *topsides*.

Cradle. A frame that supports a boat when she is not in the water.

Cranky. Difficult to steer, unstable.

Crew. In general, everybody who is helping to handle a boat. In particular, everybody on board except the *afterguard*. Used in both the singular and the plural. A "crewmember" is an individual in the crew.

Cringle. An eye in the leech ("reefing cringle"), luff ("reefing" or "Cunningham cringle"), or tack or clew ("tack" or "clew cringle") of a sail, composed of a grommet stamped into the cloth and heavily reinforced by stitching.

Crossbeam. An *athwartships* support between the *hulls* of a *multihull*.

Cross Chop. Confused pattern of waves.

Cross Cut. Describes a sail that has *panels* extending across the sail. See *Radial Clew, Radial Head*.

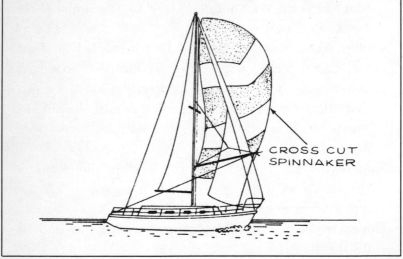

CROSS CUT SPINNAKER

Crosstrees. British for *spreaders*.

Crowd On Sail. To carry as much sail as possible.

Crown. 1) Convex curvature in a deck. 2) The point on an anchor where the arms are attached to the shank, or main body. Illustration on page 4.

Cruise. A period of time longer than one day spent for pleasure on a non-racing yacht that is under way from harbor to harbor during many of the daylight hours.

Cruiser. A boat designed and used exclusively for cruising and not racing. See *Cruise*.

Cruiser-Racer. A boat whose primary purpose is cruising but that is also capable of racing successfully. Also, "dual-purpose yacht." See *Racer-Cruiser*.

Cruising Boat. A boat used only for cruising.

Cruising Club of America. See *CCA*.

Cruising Range. The distance a boat can cover under power without refueling.

Cruising Speed. The speed under power at which the engine is working at the most economical number of revolutions per minute.

Crystallization. Structural alteration in metal that eventually leads to its failure at stress points.

Cuddy. A small cabin on a small boat that provides some protection from the wind and water in rough weather.

Cunningham. A *sail control* line leading through a *cringle* in the lower part of the sail's *luff*. To tighten the sail's luff and pull wrinkles out of the sail or move the point of deepest *camber* forward, pull down on this line.

Current. The horizontal motion of water caused by tide or wind. See *Drift, Set.*

Custom Design (Custom-Built). A boat designed (or built) specifically for one client—not a "stock" or "production" boat. Also called "one-off construction."

Cutter. A single-masted boat with the mast more than one-third of the LOA aft of the headstay, generally but not always carrying a *double-headsail rig.* In a sloop the mast is forward of that point. See *LOA.*

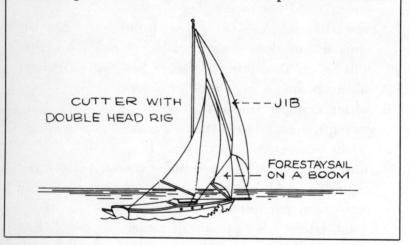

Cut Water. The forward edge of the stem.

D

Dacron. The trademarked name for the white, low-stretch, polyester fiber used to make most sails other than spinnakers and to make low-stretch rope.

Daggerboard. A plastic, wood, or metal plate that serves the same purpose as a *centerboard*. Rather than pivoting, however, it retracts vertically.

Dampen. To moderate motion.

Danger Sector. The red part of a lighthouse's light that warns of shoals in the area it covers.

Danger Signal. Five or more quick blasts of a horn or whistle.

Datum. The reference depth of water on a chart.

Davit. Small crane used to hoist a dinghy.

Daybeacon. A stake stuck at the edge of a channel with a placard ("daymark") whose color, shape, and number indicate the channel according to the *Lateral System*. Daybeacons take the place of *buoys* as *aids to navigation* in very shallow water.

Day Racing. Competition lasting only a few hours during the day.

Daysailer. A cabinless boat (though she may have a cuddy) used for short sails and racing.

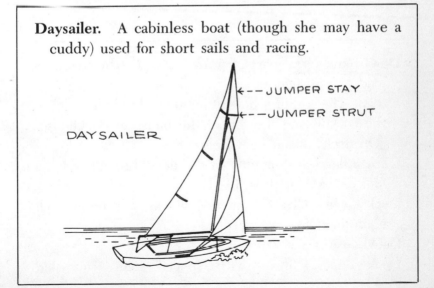

DAYSAILER

←--JUMPER STAY

←--JUMPER STRUT

Dead. Exactly, directly, for example "dead high tide," "dead ahead."

Dead-End. To secure an end of a line to a stationary object.

Dead Head. 1) A spar floating on its end and used as a mooring buoy. 2) A pile projecting above a pier.

Dead Muzzler. A strong wind from dead ahead.

Dead Reckoning (DR). The calculation and updating of a boat's *position* using as data only the boat's previous position, the *course* steered, and the distance covered. See *Fix*.

Deadrise. The angle that the underbody makes with the horizontal in an athwartships section.

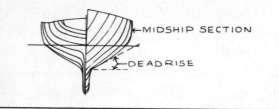

Deadwood. The part of a *keel* that does not contain lead or iron *ballast*.

Deck. The top of a hull other than the floor (sole) of the cockpit and the top of the house or deckhouse. "On deck" means "not below."

Deck Filler. An opening in the deck through which a fuel or water tank is filled.

Deck Gear. Cleats, winches, blocks, and other such equipment.

Deckhouse. See *Trunk*.

Deck Shoes. Shoes with special soles ("non-skid

soles") that grip a wet, pitching *deck*. Often called "Topsiders" after the trademarked name of one brand of shoes.

Decksweeper.　See *Low Cut*.

Deep Six.　To sink an object.

Deepwater.　Offshore.

Delivery.　A *passage* whose purpose is to get the boat to a location where she will be met by her owner.

Depower.　To make the sails more *flat*. Opposite of *Power*.

Depth.　1) "Water depth" is the distance from the surface to the *bottom*; the *datum* water depth shown on *charts* usually is the depth at *mean low water*, or the average of low *tide* levels. 2) "Sail depth" is the measurement of the sail's draft or *camber*. 3) "Boat depth" is the distance from the water to the lowest part of the boat when the boat is upright.

Depth Sounder.　An electronic device that indicates the depth of water. A "Fathometer" is a depth sounder made only by Raytheon Co. A "depth recorder" records depth on graph paper.

Deviation.　Movement of a compass card (measured in degrees West or East) resulting from the effect of metal on the boat. A "deviation card" indicates the amount of deviation at various headings.

Dinette.　An L- or U-shaped settee around two or three sides of a table that can be dropped to the settee's level to form a double berth.

Dinghy.　A small, light rowing or sailing boat. See *Pram*.

Dink.　Slang for "dinghy."

Directional Stability.　See *Stability*.

Discontinuous Shroud. A shroud (side *stay*) that consists of several distinct lengths of wire or rod running between the mast and a *spreader*, between spreaders, and between a spreader and the *deck* with a *turnbuckle* at the lower end of each length. This arrangement produces less stretch than one long shroud.

Dismasted. Describes a boat with a mast broken while she was under way.

Displacement (Disp.). A boat's weight in pounds or tons, or the volume of her underbody in cubic feet (a figure that indicates the amount of water she displaces). "Light displacement" describes a boat that is relatively lightweight for her length. "Heavy displacement" describes a boat that is relatively heavy. "Moderate displacement" describes a boat that is neither excessively light nor excessively heavy. See *Displacement/Length Ratio.*

Displacement Boat. A boat that is too heavy to lift up out of the water and *plane* in fresh wind. See *Hull Speed.*

Displacement/Length Ratio. A number that indicates a boat's displacement (weight) relative to her size. The formula has two steps. First, determine the boat's displacement in long tons by dividing her weight by 2240. Second, divide the displacement in long tons by $(.01 \times \text{waterline length})^3$. If the result is 325 or over, the boat is a heavy *cruiser*. If it is 200-325, she is a light or moderately heavy cruiser or *racer-cruiser*. If it is 200 or less, she is a very light cruiser or a light *racer*. See *Sail-Area/Displacement Ratio.*

Distance Racing. See *Ocean Racing.*

Ditty Bag. A small synthetic fabric or canvas bag used to carry a knife, light line, whipping needles, and other boatswain's gear.

Divided Rig. See *Split Rig.*

Dock. 1) To bring a boat alongside a float or pier. 2) The water between two floats or piers.

Docking Line. A line used to tie one boat to another or to a pier or float.

Documented. Describes a boat registered with the federal government rather than with a state. The boat may clear and enter U.S. ports with little paperwork and she need not carry numbers on her bow. The documentation numbers must be carved into a main beam below.

Dodger. A fold-up spray shield over a hatch.

Doghouse. A shelter forward of a cockpit or over a hatch.

Doldrums. A large calm area lying between the Northern and Southern Hemisphere trade wind belts. See *Trade Winds.*

Dollop. A small wave breaking over the rail.

Dolly. A small hand-pulled boat trailer.

Dolphin. A piling or pole used as a mooring buoy or as an aid to navigation.

Dolphin Striker. See *Bobstay.*

Dorade Ventilator. A type of ventilator that does not permit spray or small waves on deck to pass below with the fresh air. It was first used in the ocean racer *Dorade* in 1931.

Dory. A flat-bottomed rowing boat used originally as a fishing boat on the Grand Banks.

Double-Bottomed. Describes a boat whose *cockpit sole* is several inches above the boat's *bottom*. This allows water to drain out quickly so the boat may be *righted* after a *capsize*.

Double-Ender. A boat with a pointed stern. If the stern is especially wide before it closes to the point, it is called a "canoe stern."

Double-Grooved Headstay. See *Grooved Headstay, Grooved Mast*.

Double-Headsail Rig. A *sail plan* or *rig* that allows two *jibs* to be set simultaneously. The outer sail, called the "jib," is set on the headstay, and the inner jib, called the "staysail" or "forestaysail," is set on the forestay. Also, "double-head rig." See *Stay*.

Double Up. To install or rig a back-up to a piece of gear. For example, "double up the mooring line" means to rig another mooring line to take some of the load of the primary line. To "triple up" means to install or rig two back-ups.

Downeaster. A person or boat from Maine, which is downwind from and to the East of Boston.

Downhaul. A tackle that controls the height of a boom's sliding gooseneck, or a line (also called a "foreguy") that keeps a spinnaker pole from flying in the air.

Downwind. Away from the direction from which the wind is blowing. Opposite of *Upwind*. Also "offwind," "downhill."

Dowse. To lower quickly.

DR. See *Dead Reckoning*.

Draft. 1) (Dr.). The *depth* of the boat underwater. 2) The *camber* of a sail.

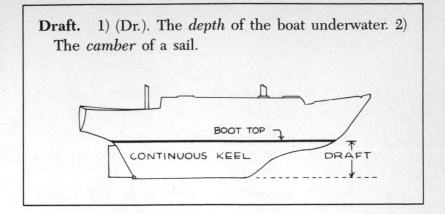

BOOT TOP

CONTINUOUS KEEL   DRAFT

Drag. 1) Resistance. 2) See *Anchor*.

Dress Ship. To display flags in honor of a holiday or an event.

Drift. The velocity of the current. See *Set*.

Drifter. A lightweight jib used when racing in extremely light wind. Sometimes called "windseeker."

Drifting Conditions. Wind of 0-3 knots. A "drifting match" is a race held in drifting conditions.

Drive. A boat's ability to sail through waves without much loss in speed.

Drogue. Any object that is dragged astern to slow the boat in *heavy weather*. Compare with *Sea Anchor*.

Dry Suit. Waterproof clothing with seals at the cuffs and neck to keep the body completely dry.

Dual-Purpose Yacht. See *Cruiser-Racer*, *Racer-Cruiser*.

DWL. Designed waterline. See *LWL*.

Dying. Describes a wind or boat whose speed is *decreasing*.

E

Earing. See *Reef*.

Ease. To reduce pressure or tension. "Ease the helm" means to reduce weather helm. When the wind or sea "eases," its force is reduced. "Ease the sheet" means to let it go a determined amount; also "let go." See *Veer*.

Easy. Smooth and without undue strain, e.g., "easy helm," "easy motion in a seaway."

Ebb. The outgoing tide; opposite of *Flood*.

Eddy. A circular current. See *Back Eddy*.

Emergency Equipment. Equipment used to repair major damage, call for help, abandon ship, rescue a *crew* who has fallen *overboard*, etc.

End for End. Reversal.

Ensign. A national flag flown from a boat. Also, *colors*.

Entry. The underbody near the bow, either Veed or U-shaped.

EPIRB. Emergency position-indicating radio beacon. Activated in an emergency, it sends a signal that can be received by satellites, aircraft, and ships, which may home in on it to locate the distressed vessel.

Eye. A loop. A "Flemish eye" is a loop sewn into the end of a *line* to enable the line to be *led* through the boom or *mast* with a *messenger*.

Eye of a Storm. The center of a storm, where it is relatively calm.

Eye of the Wind. The precise direction of the wind.

Eyes. The topsides near the bow. So called because in

ancient times, mariners believed that boats could see their way if eyes were painted on either side of the bow.

F

Fair. Smooth. Opposite of *Unfair*.

Fairlead. An eye, usually on deck or on a spar, through which a line is led, primarily to keep it from fouling another line or from chafing. A lead that is fair is a line that is not fouled or that does not chafe.

Fairway. The middle of a channel.
Fair Wind. A wind from abaft the beam that permits sailing on a broad reach or a run.
Fake. See *Flake*.
Fall. See *Part, Tackle*.
Fall Off. See *Head Off*.
Family Cruiser. A roomy easy-to-sail cruising boat.
Fast. Secure. To "make fast" is to secure.

Fastenings. The screws, nails, etc., holding a boat together.

Fastnet Gale. The storm that hit the fleet in the 1979 race from England to Fastnet Rock off Ireland and return. Fifteen sailors died in this gale—the greatest disaster in the history of pleasure boating.

Fathom. Six feet.

Fathometer. See *Depth Sounder.*

Favor. To ease or help. A "favoring wind shift" is a lift.

Federal System. See *Lateral System.*

Feeder. A device that automatically *leads* a sail's *luff* into a *grooved headstay or mast.*

Feel. A good helmsman's sense of how effectively a boat is sailing.

Fender. A padded object, made of rope, plastic, or rubber, that is hung over the topsides to protect them from abrasion by an object alongside. A "fender board" is a plank sometimes hung outboard of several fenders to improve the protection.

Fend Off. To prevent the boat from banging against another object.

Ferro Cement Construction. A boatbuilding technique in which mortar is laid over wire mesh that is reinforced by steel rods.

Fetch. 1) To clear a buoy or point of land. 2) The distance between an object and the windward shore.

Fiberglass Construction. The most popular boatbuilding technique, in which high-strength glass fibers, loose or woven in a cloth, are bonded and shaped using a glue called "resin." When the fiberglass is reinforced by balsa wood or sheets of plastic, the technique is called "cored construction" or "sandwich construction."

Fid.   In splicing line, a pointed object used to seperate strands.

Fiddle.   A strip of wood secured edgewise on a table to keep small objects from sliding in heavy weather.

Fill.   To catch wind.

Fine-Ended.   Describes a boat with sharply Veed sections under a narrow bow and stern. Opposite of *full-ended*. Illustration on page 72.

Fin Keel.   See *Keel*.

First.   There are several types of firsts in yacht races. In a handicap race, such as an ocean race, there is "first to finish," and "first overall" and "in class" for fleet and class winners on corrected time, after all boats have finished and the handicaps have been computed. In a one-design race, however, the boat that is first to finish is also first overall.

Fish.   1) To repair a broken spar by lashing "fishes," or lengths of wood or metal that serve as splints, over the fracture. 2.) To lead an internal halyard or *messenger* through a mast.

Fit-Out.   To prepare a boat for launching and sailing. "Fitting-out time" comes just before a boat is launched.

Fittings.   Small items of equipment in the *rigging*.

Fix.   The calculation of a boat's *position* using as data *bearings* or *celestial navigation* sights on two or more known objects.

Flag Officer.   A yacht club officer—commodore, vice-commodore, rear commodore, fleet captain—who has a distinctive flag that he or she may fly from his or her yacht.

Flake. To coil a line or fold a sail so it will run out easily. Also "fake."

Flake Down. To coil a line for stowage.

Flare. 1) Outward sweep of the topsides from waterline to rail. 2) A signal that can be ignited to indicate an emergency.

Flat. Describes a boat that is not heeling, a sail with very little draft (*camber*), or an extremely calm sea. There is no wind in a "flat calm."

Flat Out. Pure, as in "flat out ocean racer," a boat designed only for ocean racing.

Flattening Reef. See *Reef*.

Fleet. A group of boats.

Float. A buoyant, sturdy platform at the end of a pier, with access over a gangway or down steps, that rises and falls with the tide and to which boats are temporarily tied up.

Float Coat. A parka with buoyancy.

Flood. The incoming tide; opposite of *Ebb*.

Floors. The frames (ribs) under the cabin sole.

Floorboards. Slats for walking over the *bilge*.

Flotation. See *Buoyancy*.

Flukes. The sharp protrusions of an anchor that dig into the bottom.

Fluky. Describes a light, shifty wind.

Flush-Decked. Describes a boat with no trunk protruding from the deck and with all cabins below deck. Also, "raised decked."

Flying Jibe. See *Jibe*.

Fog. Condensed water vapor near the water or land that causes poor visibility. It is caused by warm air passing over cold water or by cold air passing over warm water. "Fog signals" are horns, bells, whistles, or cannon sounded from vessels or lighthouses during periods of poor visibility.

Following Sea. Waves from astern.

Foot. 1) The lower edge of a sail. 2) "Footing": To sail close-hauled, with little regard for pointing, in an attempt to maximize speed. See *Point*.

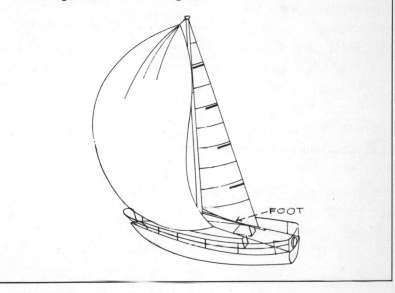

Foot Block. See *Block*.

Foot Line. A line that adjusts a sail's tension along its *foot*.

Force. An indicator of wind and sea conditions used in the Beaufort Scale e.g., "Force 7 gale." See *Beaufort Scale*.

Fore. Abbreviation for "forward" used as a prefix or adjective to denote location toward the *bow*, for example "forebody" (the front portion of the *hull* beneath the water).

Fore and Aft. Specifically, in line with the keel; frequently also means "all over the boat."

Foredeck. The *deck* between the *mast* and the *bow.*

Forefoot. The most forward part of the underbody. A "deep forefoot" is relatively deep in the water below the waterline. A "shallow (or cutaway) forefoot" turns aft toward the keel just below the waterline.

Foreguy. See *Guy.*

Forepeak. A stowage compartment in the very forward part of the boat.

Forereach. To sail slowly almost into the wind with the sails mostly *luffing.*

Foresail. See *Jib.*

Forestay. See *Stay.*

Forestaysail. See *Jibe.*

Foretriangle. The area bounded by the mast below the hounds, the headstay, and the foredeck between the mast and the headstay.

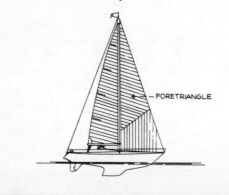

— FORETRIANGLE

Forgiving. Describes a boat that will not readily *capsize* or *broach* when sailed inexpertly. Compare with *Seakindly, Seaworthy*.

Forward. Toward the bow. "Forward of the beam" is the area between dead abeam and dead ahead. Illustration on page 3.

Foul. 1) Describes a tangled line, an anchor tangled in its rode, or a boat's bottom that is covered with weed or barnacles; also an unfavorable current. 2) To hit another boat illegally or force her to alter course by violating a racing rule.

Foul Weather Gear. Trousers, jackets, boots, and hats that protect the wearer from rain and spray. Also called "oilers" (because they used to be made of oilskin) and "slickers."

Found. Furnished. "Well found" means "well furnished" or "well equipped."

Founder. To swamp or to sink.

Fractional Rig. A *sail plan* in which the headstay intersects the *mast* part-way down from the top. Opposite of *masthead rig*. See *Masthead*.

Frame. Part of the skeleton structure of a boat; transverse ribs.

Frap. To bind or draw together with rope.

Free. 1) Describes sailing on a broad *reach* or a run. 2) A "freeing" wind is one that "fairs" or shifts aft.

Freeboard. The height of the topsides.

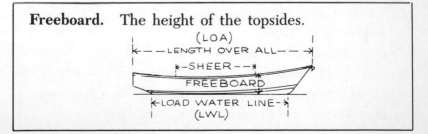

Freshen.   1) Increase in the wind speed. 2) To head up while on a downwind leg, e.g., from a run to a broad *reach*.

Fresh Wind.   Wind of 16-22 knots.

Front.   See *Low-Pressure System*.

Frostbiting.   Dinghy racing in northern areas during the late fall, winter, and early spring.

Full and By.   Sailing close-hauled with all sails full.

Full-Ended.   Describes a hull with U-shaped, well-rounded, and relatively large bow and stern sections. Opposite of *Fine-Ended*. Illustration on page 72.

Full Sail.   With all sails set and not *reefed*.

Furl.   To *flake* or roll up sails on a *boom* or *stay*. See *Roller Furler*.

G

Gadget.   A small and specialized piece of gear. See *Gear*.

Gaff-Rigged.   Describes a boat with a four-sided mainsail (instead of triangular, as on a marconi rig). The top side is supported by a spar (the "gaff"). This was the usual rig on yachts until the 1920s. Illustration on page 101.

Gale.   See *Beaufort Scale*.

Galley.   The cooking and food-storage area in a boat.

Gallows Frame.   A heavy permanently installed support for the main boom.

Gam.   To tell sea stories; a storytelling session.

Gangway.   1) An opening in a rail or lifeline to facilitate boarding (also, "boarding gate"). 2) A ramp from a pier to a float.

Garboard Strake.   The plank or plating in the underbody near the keel of a wooden or metal boat.

Gasket.   See *Sail Stop.*

Gear.   Generic term for all running rigging and other non-permanent equipment, e.g., "foul weather gear," "boatswain's gear," "genoa gear." A mast is not a piece of gear; a masthead fly is.

Gear Buster.   A race or passage in weather so heavy that damage is risked.

Genoa.   A jib whose clew is trimmed well aft of the mast and overlaps the mainsail. Nicknamed "genny."

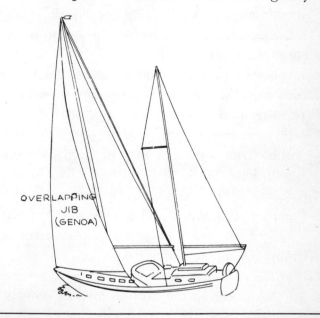

OVERLAPPING
JIB
(GENOA)

Gilguy. A light line that holds a halyard away from a mast when at anchor or mooring.

Gilhickey. A makeshift, otherwise unnamed gadget.

Gimbals. Supports permitting a table, stove, or berth to pivot as the boat heels so that its top remains level.

Give. 1) Stretch in a line or bend in a spar. 2) To "give way" is to avoid a collision with another boat.

Give-Way Vessel. A boat or ship required by the rules of the road to alter course when a collision threatens. Opposite of *Stand-On Vessel*. Once called "burdened vessel."

Glass. See *Barometer*.

Go About. To tack.

Gold Plater. A very expensive boat.

Gong Buoy. See *Buoy*.

Gooseneck. The metal fitting that secures the boom to the mast. It is a "sliding gooseneck" if it slides on a track on the mast, altering tension on the sail's luff.

Goosewing Jibe. See *Jibe*.

Government Mark. A buoy set by the Coast Guard or some other government agency to serve as an aid to navigation.

Grab Rail (Strap). A length of perforated wood, webbing, or rope that may be held by a crewmember to keep her or his balance. Also, "handrail."

Gradient. The "steepness," or distance between the barometric *isobars*. The closer the isobars, the "steeper" the gradient; hence, the stronger the wind.

Granny. A mistied square knot.

Grapnel. A four-pronged anchor used for short stops and for dragging the bottom for lost objects.

Grommet. A metal ring punched or sewn into a sail,

at the head, tack, and clew. A grommet is part of a *cringle*.

Grooved Headstay, Grooved Mast. A system for setting sails that provides a small groove into which a sail's luff is inserted and pulled up by a halyard. This system replaces hanks for the jib and slides for the mainsail or mizzen. A "double-grooved headstay" allows a new jib to be set before the old one is lowered.

Ground. 1) To run aground. 2) To secure a wire against short-circuiting.

Groundswell. Long waves that run almost continuously due to steady winds.

Ground Tackle. Anchors and anchor rodes and chain.

Gudgeon. An eye-shaped device secured to a transom that receives the pintle on a rudder.

Gunkhole. A narrow, shallow area of water.

Gunwale. See *Rail*.

Guy. A line used to position a spar, usually a spinnaker pole. The "afterguy" controls the spar's fore and aft position, while the "foreguy" prevents it from lifting.

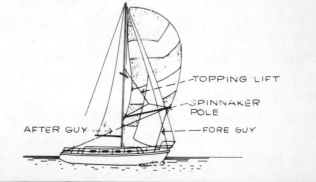

TOPPING LIFT

SPINNAKER POLE

AFTER GUY

FORE GUY

Gust. A strong puff of wind.

Gybe. See *Jibe*.

H

Halyard. A wire or low-stretch *line* that pulls up and holds up a sail. An "internal halyard" is led partly inside the *mast* to reduce windage.

Halyard Stopper. See *Lock-Off*.

Hand. 1) A *crewmember*. 2) A side, for example "*starboard* hand." 3) To lower a sail.

Hand-Bearing Compass. See *Compass*.

Handicap. See *Rating Rule*.

Handrails. See *Grab Rail (Strap)*.

Hand Signals. Visual commands made when verbal commands are inaudible. Among the common signals are: point forward ("*ease sheet*"); point aft ("*trim sheet*"); point up ("*hoist* the sail"); point down ("*dowse* the sail"); point to windward ("*head up*"); point to leeward ("*head off*"); show open palm ("stop").

Handsomely. Carefully, gradually, and in a seamanlike manner.

Handy. 1) Close at hand. 2) Describes a boat that tacks quickly.

Hanging Locker. Closet.

Hank. A hook that secures a *jib* to a *stay*. A "piston hank," which is normally used, has a pistonlike spring-loaded retaining pin. To "hank on" a jib is to prepare a jib for sailing.

Happy Hour. A short period of relaxation aboard an ocean cruising or ocean racing yacht, usually in the late afternoon.

Harbor Master. The official who enforces port regulations, supervises mooring, docking, etc. Also, "port captain."

Hard. 1) "The hard" is a stone, concrete, or other firm area of the water's bottom that is exposed at low *tide*. A boat is intentionally *grounded* there at high tide so that she may be painted after the tide goes out. 2) Full (sail). 3) Strong (wind).

Hard Alee. See *Alee*.

Harden. To trim a sail.

Harden Up. See *Head Up*.

Hard Over. To put the helm as far as possible in one direction. "Hard down" is all the way to leeward; "hard up" is all the way to windward.

Hardware. Generic term for cleats, winches, blocks, and other metal and plastic gear.

Hatch. Opening in a deck; it is covered by a hatch cover.

Haul (Hauling). 1) To pull. 2) See *Veer*.

Hawsepipe. A pipe passing through the foredeck through which the anchor rode passes overboard.

Hazard to Navigation. A shallow area, rock, wrecked ship, drifting vessel, or other obstruction in the water.

Head. 1) Toilet room on a boat. 2) The upper corner of a sail. Illustration on page 8. 3) To aim a boat in a direction, e.g., "head into the wind." 4) The bow.

Headboard. The reinforcement at the head of a mainsail or mizzen.

Header. A wind shift that requires the helmsman to

head off to keep the sails full. The opposite of *Lift*.

Heading. See *Course*.

Head Off. To change course away from the wind. Also, "bear away," "bear off," "come off," "fall off."

Headroom. The height of a cabin. "Standing headroom" is about 6'2", since it permits most people to stand without stooping in a cabin. "Sitting headroom" is much less and permits most people only to sit on a bunk and crouch.

Headsail. See *Jib*.

Head Sea, Head Wind. Large waves or wind from ahead. Also, "on the nose."

Headstay. See *Stay*.

Head to Wind. Describes a boat heading directly into the wind.

Head Up. To change course toward the wind. Also, "harden up," "come up."

Headway. A boat's forward motion.

Heave. To throw.

Heave-To. To sail a boat very slowly (usually under *shortened sail*) with the wind 50-60 degrees off the bow, riding comfortably and making only about one knot without the need for a steerer. "Hove-To" describes a boat that is heaving-to.

Heavily Built. Unusually strongly constructed.

Heaving Line. A light *line* that can be easily thrown to another boat or to a swimmer needing rescue.

Heavy Air. A near-gale, with winds of 27-34 knots.

Heavy Displacement. See *Displacement*.

Heavy Seas. Extremely high waves.

Heavy Weather. Conditions in which high wind and large waves make sailing difficult if not dangerous.

Also "hard weather," "rough weather."

Heel. The degree to which the boat tips, or cants, to leeward under the force of the wind in the sails.

Heeling Force. The wind pressure that causes a boat to heel.

Helm. 1) The steering gear on a boat. 2) Describes the way a boat is balanced, usually as a synonym for "weather helm": the tendency of a boat to round up into the wind when the tiller or wheel is released. "Lee helm" is the tendency to head off away from the wind. See *Balanced*.

Helmsman. See *Steerer*.

Helmsmanship. The ability to steer a boat well.

Hike. 1) For the crew of a small boat to lean backward over the windward rail to help keep the boat from heeling (also, "hike out"). To "minihike" is to hike with the body in a Z-like configuration, sitting on the topsides. 2) In some areas, a synonym for "heel."

High.   Sailing too close to the wind ("pinching"; see *Pinch*).

High Cut.   Describes a jib whose clew is relatively high off the deck.

High Performance.   Describes an especially fast, usually planing, small boat. See *Planing Boat*.

High Pressure.   Relatively high atmospheric pressure. A "high pressure system" generally includes dry, calm weather.

High-Water Mark.   The line of debris or weed made on the shore at the average high-water level.

Hiking Power.   The leverage a crew exerts to counteract heeling force. It is a function of crew weight, agility, and endurance.

Hiking Stick.   See *Tiller*.

Hiking Strap.   A length of webbing in the cockpit under which the crew's toes are hooked for support while he *hikes*.

Hitch.   Turns in a line to secure it to a *spar* or *stay*. See *Bend, Knot*.

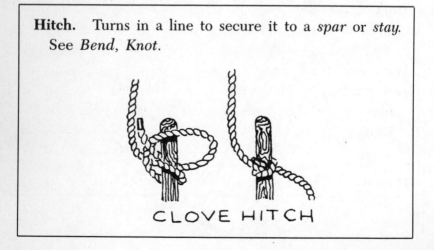

CLOVE HITCH

Hockle.   A tight kink in a line.

Hogged.   Describes a boat whose bow and stern have drooped, generally because they are unsupported when the boat rests in a cradle.

Hoist.   1) To raise a sail. 2) The length of a sail's *luff*.

Holding Ground.   The type of bottom in which a boat is anchored. A "good holding ground" provides a strong bite for the anchor *flukes*; it is usually mud or clay. A "poor holding ground" is usually composed of fine-grained sand or rock.

Holding Tank.   Onboard sewage storage tank that is pumped out at a shore facility.

Hole.   See *Lull*.

Home Port.   The usual berth of a ship when she is in commission.

Hook.   Slang for "anchor."

Hooked Leech.   A leech that takes an abrupt turn to *windward* or *leeward* instead of lying flat, as it should.

Horse Latitudes.   Regions of high pressure and light and variable winds on the periphery of the trade wind belt.

Horseshoe Ring.   See *Life Ring*.

Hot Bunks.   Berths constantly in use by crewmembers not standing a watch during an ocean passage or race.

Hounds.   The point on the mast where the jib halyard sheave is located.

HOUNDS →

House.   See *Trunk*.

Hove-To.   See *Heave-To*.

Hull.   The shell of a boat.

Hull Speed.   The potential maximum speed of a non-planing boat, measured by multiplying by 1.34 the square root of the length of the waterline.

Hull-To-Deck Joint.   The seam where the *hull* is attached to the *deck*.

Hydraulic Adjustor.   A device that uses a hydraulic ram to adjust a piece of gear, for example, a *stay* or the *vang*.

Hydrodynamics.   The study of the flow of liquids around objects.

I

Iceboat. A sailboat with "skates" that glides on ice at extremely high speeds.

In. One sails "in," not "on," a boat.

Inboard. 1) Toward the centerline of a boat. 2) In the boat.

Inflatable. Capable of being inflated by human breath, bellows, or CO_2 cartridges. Life rafts, many dinghies, some life rings, and some life jackets are inflatable.

-ing. A suffix added to the name of a cardinal point to indicate distance made good in a direction; e.g., "Easting" is distance made good to the East.

In Irons. Headed directly into the wind with no headway, so the boat cannot bear off on either tack. Also, "in stays."

Initial Stability. See *Stability.*

Inland Rules of the Road. See *Rules of the Road.*

Inlet. A narrow opening in a shoreline, providing a channel into a harbor.

Inshore. Toward the land. Opposite of *offshore.*

Interior. A boat's cabin area.

Internal Halyard. See *Halyard.*

International Code. Signal flags for letters and numbers.

International Measurement System (IMS). A *rating rule* for boats used in *offshore* races. Originally called the "Measurement Handicap System."

International Offshore Rule (IOR). A *rating rule* for boats used in *offshore* races.

International Rules of the Road (COLREGS). See *Rules of the Road.*

International Yacht Racing Union (IYRU). The governing body of all sailboat racing. It administers the *racing rules*, selects *classes* for the Olympics, and supervises the construction of many types of racing boats.

Islet. Small island.

Isobar. On a weather map, a line marking points on the earth's surface where barometer readings are the same. See *Barometer, Gradient.*

J

J. *In rating rules*, the term for the distance between

the *mast* and the *headstay,* i.e., the base length of the *foretriangle.*

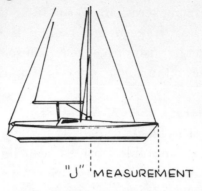

"J" MEASUREMENT

Jack.   Handy, useful. Generally used as a prefix, e.g., "jack stay."

Jackline.   A line or wire laid *fore and aft* on the *decks* and secured at the *bow* and *stern.* The *crew* hook their *safety* harnesses onto it when going on deck.

Jerry Can.   A two-to-five-gallon container, usually plastic.

Jetty.   See *Breakwater.*

Jib.   A triangular sail set on (secured to) the *headstay* or *forestay* and trimmed by a jib *sheet.* Illustrations on pages 34 and 51. If it greatly overlaps the mainsail, it is a *genoa* jib. If it barely overlaps the mast, it is a "lapper." If it does not overlap, it is called a "working jib" when set on the headstay and a "forestaysail" when set on the forestay. A "jib topsail" is set high on the headstay. Jibs are often assigned numbers to indicate relative size, with No. 1 the largest and No. 3 or greater the smallest. Jibs are attached with *hanks* or by inserting the luff into a *grooved headstay.* Also "foresail," "headsail."

Jib Boom. A boom for a jib.

Jibe. To change *tacks* by *heading off* (*downwind*) until the sails swing across the boat. In a "flying jibe," the sails are not *trimmed* in far enough and they bang across dangerously; this may cause a "goosewing jibe," where the *boom* or a *batten* hangs up on a *stay*.

Jib-Headed Rig. See *Marconi Rig*.

Jib Lead. The *block* on *deck* that the *jib sheet* passes through. A "movable jib lead" can be adjusted *fore and aft* and/or *athwartships*. See *Car*.

Jib Sheet. See *Sheet*.

Jiffy Reef. See *Reef*.

Jig. A short *tackle*.

Jigger. See *Mizzen*.

Jog Along. To sail slowly.

Joinerwork. Woodwork in a yacht's interior.

Judge. See *Racing Rules*.

Jumper Strut. A strut on the forward side of the mast, near the hounds. The jumper stay leads over it and gives fore-and-aft support to the upper mast. See *Stay*. Illustration on page 35.

Junior Program. A sailing-instruction course for children under eighteen.

Jury. See *Racing Rules*.

Jury Rig. An expedient solution to a rigging problem.

K

Kedging Anchor. A light anchor used for temporary

halts. Sometimes "lunch anchor" or "lunch hook."

Keel.   A fixed or (rarely) retractable heavy fin under the *hull* providing weight for *stability* and lateral area to resist leeway. A "keel boat" is any boat with a keel. A "keel centerboarder" is a keel boat that has a small *centerboard*. A "continuous" or "full-length" keel runs much of the length of the boat and is attached to the *rudder*. A "fin keel" is short and separate from the rudder. A "winged keel" has short winglets that improve the keel's efficiency. A "Scheel keel" is relatively shallow and has a large bulb at its bottom to improve efficiency. An "elliptical keel" (used mainly on racing boats) is shaped like an ellipse. An "upside-down keel" (usually with wings) is shorter at its top than at its bottom. "Twin keels" or "bilge keels" come in a pair, with one short keel on either side of the boat's *bottom*.

Ketch.   A two-masted sailboat with the after mast smaller than the forward one and located over or forward of the *rudder* post.

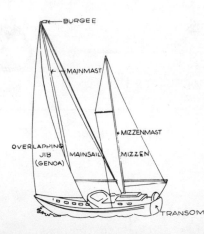

65

Kevlar. A trademarked name for a brown synthetic material used to make extremely low-stretch *sails* and *rope*.

Kicking Strap. See *Vang*.

Kink. A twist in a line that prohibits it from rendering, or running through a block.

Kite. Slang for "spinnaker."

Knock. Slang for "header."

Knockdown. Sudden and extreme heeling due to a strong gust of wind.

Knot. 1) Technically, turns in a *line* that do not involve another line or object, but generally understood to include all types of *bend* and *hitch* as well. 2) Speed of one *nautical* mile (6076 feet, or 1.15 statute mile) per hour.

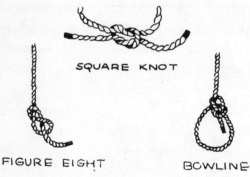

SQUARE KNOT

FIGURE EIGHT

BOWLINE

Knotmeter. See *Speedometer*.

L

Laboring. Describes a boat whose progress through waves is slow and whose motion is uncomfortable.

Laid Rope. See *Rope.*

Land Breeze. A wind whose direction is from land to sea, usually when the water is warmer than the land; also, "shore breeze." See *Sea Breeze.*

Landfall. Sighting of land at sea; usually, the first sighting after a voyage.

Lanyard. A short length of *light line* used to *secure* an object such as a knife or to operate a movable object such as a *shackle* pin.

Lapper. See *Jib.*

Lapstrake Construction. Each wooden plank overlaps the one beneath it. Also, "clinker-planked."

Lash Down. Tie down.

Lateen-Rigged. A boat with a triangular sail extended by a long spar, usually slung to a low mast.

Lateral Resistance. See *Leeway.*

Lateral System. The *buoyage* system of *aids to navigation* that predominates in North America, as different from the *cardinal system.* Here, the sides of channels are marked by *buoys* and *daybeacons.* The rule is "red right returning": on entering a smaller *body of water*, pass with the red buoys on the *starboard* side and the green or black ones on the *port* side.

Launch. 1) A small powerboat that ferries people from a pier to their boats. 2) To put a boat in the water.

Lay. A utility word. To "lay up" is to prepare a boat for storage. To "lay out gear" is to prepare equipment for use. To "lay" a buoy, course, mark, point of land, etc. is to be able to sail directly to it without having to alter *course*; the *compass direction* to the objective is called the "lay line." A "lay day" is a day off from sailing. A "layout" is an arrangement of a boat's furniture or equipment.

Lazarette. A *locker* in the *aft* part of the *cockpit* or *deck*.

Lazy. Not in use, e.g., "lazy guy": the slack one of two sheets led to the clew of a spinnaker on a large boat.

Lazy Jacks. *Lines* led between the *boom* and *mast* to cradle the *mainsail* or *mizzen* as it is lowered.

Lead. 1) Pronounced "leed": to put a line where it can be used, for example to put a docking line in a chock. 2) Pronounced "leed": a fairlead or block. 3) Pronounced "led": abbreviation for *Lead Line*.

Lead Line. A length of *light line* marked at regular intervals used to determine the water *depth*. The lead weight on the end may have tallow on its base for taking a sample of the *bottom*; this can help a *navigator*, since bottom types are indicated on many *charts*.

Lee. Abbreviation for "leeward."

Leeboard. A centerboard-type device hung not from the centerline but well outboard near the rail, as one of a pair. Found mainly in scows.

Lee Bow. 1) The leeward side of a bow. 2) To tack just below another boat's leeward bow in order to backwind her sails. 3) To "lee bow the tide" is to have the current pushing the boat to windward.

Leech. The aftermost edge of a sail, between the head and the clew; spinnaker "leeches" are the two edges between the head and clews. Illustration on page 8.

Leech Line. A light adjustable line sewn into a sail's leech. It can be tightened or loosened to control the leech's flutter.

Lee Helm. See *Helm*.

Lee Ho. English equivalent of "hard alee"—the command when tacking.

Lee Shore. A coastline onto which the wind is blowing from the water.

Leeward, Lee. Away from the wind; downwind. Leeward is pronounced "LOO-ward." See *Windward*.

Leeway. The distance that a boat slides to leeward while she is sailing, due to the force of the wind. Leeway is counteracted by the "lateral resistance" that is a function of the size and shape of the boat's underbody and keel.

Leg. A side of a racing course, between two buoys; a part of a cruise.

Length. See *LOA, LWL*.

Let Go. To anchor.

Let Out. See *Ease*.

Level Racing. Competition between ocean racers of the same *rating*. International competition of this type is held in several "ton" categories (with "ton" reflecting the name of the original trophy): One Ton, Three-Quarter Ton, Half Ton, and Quarter Ton.

Life Jacket. A buoyant vest used to keep its wearer afloat in the water. See *PFD*.

Lifeline. A plastic-coated wire that encircles the deck, several feet above the rail, running from one support (stanchion) to another, and used as a handhold in dangerous conditions. Illustration on page 8.

Life Raft. An inflatable rubber raft or boat, carried on deck or in a readily accessible locker below.

Life Ring. A circular or horseshoe-shaped PFD designed to be thrown to somebody in the water.

Lifesling. A patented device for recovering people who have fallen overboard.

Lift. 1) A wind shift that permits a higher heading— the opposite of *header*. 2) Abbreviation for "topping lift."

Light. 1) The illumination on a lighthouse or lighted buoy. 2) Describes a sail that is luffing or a boat that is being steered too close to the wind. Also, "soft."

Light Characteristics. See *Characteristics*.

Light Displacement. See *Displacement*.

Lighted Buoy. See *Buoy*.

Lighthouse. A building on the shore or water that shows a conspicuous light that serves as an aid to navigation at night. A fog signal may also be made.

Light Line. Line whose diameter is a quarter-inch or less.

Light List. A U.S. government publication listing all lighted buoys, lighthouses, and fog signals.

Light Wind. Wind less than 8 knots.

Light Sail. See *Sail*.

Limber Hole. Hole drilled through the frames to permit water to flow to the deepest part of the bilge, where the bilge pump's intake is located.

Line. 1) A length of rope used for a particular purpose—the only "rope" on a boat is the bolt rope. 2) Abbreviation for "starting line" or "finishing line."

Line Drawings. The *yacht designer's* two-dimensional drawings showing the outline of a boat's shape in sections (fore and aft, athwartships, and parallel to the waterline). Offsets are taken from these drawings, and "lofted" (blown up to full size) by the builder. Illustration on page 72.

Line Honors. First to finish a race.

Line of Position (LOP). A compass bearing or other charted line or curve that represents a boat's general presumed location. To determine how far down the LOP the boat is positioned, cross the LOP with another LOP. The result is a *fix*.

Lines. Designed shape of a boat. A boat with "sweet lines" is a handsome, well-designed boat. When a boat "floats on her lines," she is floating as her designer intended her to.

List. The leaning of a boat resulting from greater weight on one side than the other.

LOA. Length overall. The on-deck length of a boat from transom to stem.

Locker. A *stowage* area in a boat, for example, "chain locker," "sail locker."

Lock-Off. A device consisting of a lever with metal or plastic teeth. When the lever is activated, the teeth dig into and secure a *line* under load, thereby taking the place of a *cleat*. Also called "sheet stopper," "halyard stopper," "stopper."

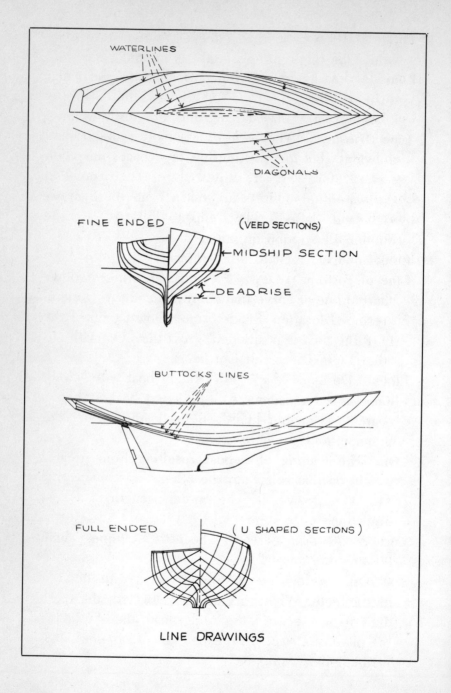

WATERLINES

DIAGONALS

FINE ENDED   (VEED SECTIONS)

←MIDSHIP SECTION

DEADRISE

BUTTOCKS LINES

FULL ENDED   (U SHAPED SECTIONS)

LINE DRAWINGS

Loft. 1) Abbreviation for "sail loft." 2) See *Line Drawings*.

Log. A device that records the mileage a boat has covered.

Log Book. A book in which the crew records observations concerning all activities of importance and general interest in and around the boat, including the weather and the boat's *speed*, *course*, and *position*.

Longitudinal. Fore and aft; parallel to the centerline.

Longshore. See *Alongshore*.

Lookout. A *crewmember* watching for danger.

Loose. Slack or baggy, for example "loose leech." Opposite of *tight*.

LOP. See *Line of Position*.

Loran-C. An electronic *navigation* system in which an onboard instrument receives signals from paired radio transmitters, calculates the time difference in reception, and computes and displays the boat's *position* either in *latitude* and *longitude* or in "time difference" (TD) lines.

Lounge. See *Saloon*.

Low. Sailing too far off the wind.

Low Cut. Describes a sail whose clew and foot are near deck. If the foot touches the deck, the sail is called a "decksweeper."

Low-Pressure System. An area in which the atmospheric pressure is lower than normal. Wind and rain occur throughout the eastern part—or "front"—of the system. Generally, the lower the atmospheric pressure, the worse the weather. Often abbreviated "low."

Lubber's Lines. Posts in a *compass* that indicate the

boat's *course* as well as *compass directions* forty-five and ninety degrees either side of the course.

Luff. 1) To alter course toward the wind, to *head up.* 2) The forward side of a sail, between the head and the tack (on a spinnaker, the side between the head and the spinnaker pole). Illustration on page 8. 3) A sail is said to luff when it is partially or entirely shaking with no wind in it. 4) A "luffing match" involves one racing boat's altering her course to prevent another from passing to windward.

Luff Groove. See *Grooved Headstay, Grooved Mast.*

Luff Hollow. The concave curve that sailmakers build into the luffs of jibs to compensate for sag in the headstay.

Luff Round (Curve). The convex curve that sailmakers build into the luffs of mainsails to compensate for mast bend.

Lull. A temporary decrease of wind velocity. Also, "hole."

LWL. Load waterline. The distance between the forwardmost and the aftermost points of a boat that are in contact with the water when she is at rest and normally equipped. Also "DWL" (Designed Waterline).

M

Mackinac Races. Annual races to Mackinac Island, Michigan, from Chicago, Illinois, and Port Huron, Michigan. Mackinac is pronounced "Mackinaw."

Made. Verbal report that something is "made fast." See *Make*, Def. No. 5.

Magnetic Direction. A direction shown in magnetic degrees on a compass rose on a chart or on the dial of a compass with no deviation. See *True Direction*.

Main. 1) Abbreviation for "mainsail." 2) Prefix meaning "primary" or "longest," for example "main companionway."

Mainmast. The largest mast on a multimasted boat. Illustration on page 65.

Mainsail. Pronounced "mains'l." The principal sail on the mainmast. Illustration on page 65.

Main Sheet. See *Sheet*.

Make. 1) See *Fetch*, Def. No. 1. 2) To "make land on another boat" is to sail faster than another boat so that the land appears to be moving behind her. 3) To "make sail" is to *set* or *hoist* the sails. 4) To "make colors" is to raise the *ensign* at 0800 hrs. (8 A.M.) 5) To "make fast" is to secure a line.

Man. For a crewmember to get in position to work at a job.

Manoverboard. When a *crewmember* falls over the side into the water. "Manoverboard gear" is the *emergency equipment* used in the rescue. A "manoverboard drill" is a practice session with this gear.

Marconi Rig. The modern sailing rig, with a three-sided mainsail (instead of the four-sided one found on gaff-rigged sailing vessels). So called because its height and complexity looked (to sailors in the 1920s) like a wireless transmitter. Also called "Bermudian" or "jib-headed" rig.

Marina. A place where boats not in use are secured to *floats* and *piers*.

Marine. Relating to the sea or boats, e.g., "marine biology," "marine insurance," "marine blue." A marine, traditionally, was an experienced seaman.

Maritime. Of or to do with commercial seafaring.

Mark. 1) A *buoy*, island, or other object that defines a *race* course. 2) A verbal report given by the *steerer* that the boat is on *course*.

Marline. A tarred *light line*.

Marline Spike. A pointed steel tool used for opening jammed knots, leading rope strands while splicing, starting holes, etc. A yachtsman's knife usually has one.

Mast. A wood, aluminum, or fiberglass pole standing vertically in a sailboat and on which sails are set.

Mast Bend. The direction and amount of bend in a mast when sails are full.

Mast Boot. A rubber seal around the *mast* at the *partners* (at *deck* level) that prevents water from dripping below.

Mast Butt. The bottom end of the mast.

Masthead. The top of the *mast*. In a "masthead rig," the *jib halyard* is at the masthead, as opposite from *fractional rig*.

Masthead Fly. A wind-direction indicator on top of the mast.

Mast Step. The support for the bottom of the *mast* fastened in the *bilge* or on *deck*.

Match Race. A race between only two boats.

Maxi Boat. An *offshore racing* boat about 80 feet

LOA that has the highest *rating* (70 feet) allowed by the *International Offshore Rule (IOR)*. Abbreviated "maxi."

Mayday. International radiotelephone distress signal. (From the French *"M'aider"*—"Help me.")

Mean High Water (MHW), Mean Low Water (MLW). The average water *depth* at high and low *tide*.

Measurement Rule. See *Rating Rule*.

Messenger. A light line used to haul a heavier line or wire rope; usually led through a block on a *spar* or thrown from boat to pier.

Midget Ocean Racing Club (MORC). An organization that sponsors a *rating rule* and races for *racer-cruisers* smaller than thirty feet.

Midships. See *Amidships*.

Midships Cockpit Layout. An accommodations plan for a cruising boat in which the cockpit is forward of or over a cabin, though not usually dead amidships. Also, "after cabin" and "center cockpit" layout.

Midships Section. The line drawings of the cross-section of the middle of the boat—halfway between bow and stern. Illustration on page 72.

Midwinters. A one-design class's winter championship.

Millibar (Mb.). A unit of atmospheric pressure, equal to 1/1000 of a bar, or 1000 dynes per square centimeter. One mb. is equivalent to .03 inch of mercury; 1016 mb. is the equivalent of 30 inches. See *Barometer*.

Minute. One-sixtieth of a degree. On Mercator Projection *charts*, one minute of *latitude* (the side of the chart) equals one *nautical* mile.

Mizzen.   The aftermost sail on a *ketch* or *yawl*, hung aft of the *mizzenmast*. A "mizzen staysail" is a light nylon reaching sail set forward of the mizzenmast; a "mizzen spinnaker" is a spinnaker set forward of the mizzenmast when running; a "mizzen genoa" is a jiblike Dacron sail set forward of the mizzenmast when close-hauled or close-reaching. Also, "jigger." Illustration on page 65.

Moderate Wind.   Wind of 9-15 knots.

Mole.   A pierlike loading and discharging place in a port. See *Breakwater*.

Monkey's Fist.   A large round *knot* that provides weight at the throwing end of a *heaving line*.

Monohull.   A boat with one hull. See *Multihull*.

Mooring.   A permanently set *anchor* or heavy weight (for example, an old automobile engine or a cement block) with a strong *rode* connected to a *bouy* to be picked up by a boat. A boat on a mooring is "moored."

Motion.   The degree of comfort on a boat sailing in *heavy weather*. A boat with an "easy motion" is comfortable.

Motor.   See *Power*, Def. No. 2.

Motor Sailer.   An *auxiliary* with an especially large engine and a relatively small *sail plan*.

Multihull.   A boat with two or three hulls—a catamaran or trimaran. The opposite of *monohull*.

Mylar.   A stiff material used to construct low-stretch sails.

N

Narrows. A narrow body of water, frequently between an island and the mainland.

Nautical. Pertaining to ships, boats, navigation, and sailors. A "nautical mile" is 1.15 statute mile. See *Knot*.

Nav. Abbreviation for "navigator." A "nav station" is the navigator's station.

Naval Architect. A designer of ships and boats.

Navigable. Describes areas where boats can be sailed without facing constant risk of running aground.

Navigation. The science of conducting a boat from one port to another.

Navigation Lights. Onboard lights to be used when under way at night, required by the *rules of the road*. Also, "running lights."

Navigator. The *crewmember* assigned to determining and keeping track of the boat's *position* and calculating which *courses* should be sailed.

Navigator's Station. The *chart* table and the surrounding area and instruments where the *navigator* does her or his work. Abbreviated "nav station."

Neap Tide. See *Tide*.

Non-Skid. Describes an object with a special surface that resists skidding and slipping, for example "non-skid shoe sole," "non-skid deck," "non-skid plates and bowls." See *Deck Shoes*.

Nor'easter. A Northeaster. Generally, a three-day storm, wind, or gale from the Northeast and East.

Norther. A two- or three-day strong North wind, bringing cold temperatures to the Deep South during the winter.

Northwester. A cool breeze from the Northwest; in the U.S., except on the Pacific Coast, it is extremely shifty.

Notice to Mariners. A weekly government publication that announces the appearance of *hazards*, changes in *buoys*, and other news of interest to sailors. It appears in two forms: the national *Notice to Mariners*; and ten regional editions of *Local Notice to Mariners*.

Nun Buoy. See *Buoy, Lateral System.*

Nylon. A synthetic fiber used in making strong, stretchy line (generally used for mooring and anchoring) and cloth (for spinnakers and other light sails).

O

Obstruction. Any object requiring a boat to make a major course alteration to pass to one side or another.

Ocean Passage. A nonstop voyage covering a long distance offshore. Also, "voyage."

Ocean (Offshore) Racing. Competition between boats with accommodations (berths, a galley, etc.) that generally is longer than one day and that takes place at least several miles from land. *Rating rules* are used to handicap boats of different sizes. Also called "distance" or "long-distance" racing. Boats that take part in these races are known as "ocean" or "offshore racers."

Offshore. Well away from shore, *off soundings.*

Off Soundings. Offshore beyond the hundred-fathom depth mark.

Off Wind. See *Downwind.* Also, "before the wind."

Oil Bag. A sack with holes through which oil is dripped overboard to calm rough seas.

Oilcanning. See *Panting.*

Oilers, Oilskins. See *Foul Weather Gear.*

Old Man. Slang for "the man in charge," the captain or skipper.

On. See *In.*

On (Off) Course. See *Course.*

Onboard. In or on a boat.

One-Design. A racing boat whose rigging and hull shape, construction, and weight are rigidly controlled. All like boats must conform to class measurement rules.

One Off. See *Custom Design.*

On Even Keel. Describes a boat that is not heeling or leaning.

On Soundings. Inshore of the hundred-fathom depth mark.

On the Beam. See *Abeam.*

On the Bow (Stern). Four points (forty-five degrees) or less either side of the bow (stern).

On the Nose. See *Head Sea, Head Wind.*

On the Run. Quickly, without pausing. To let a halyard go on the run is to let it down without snubbing it.

On the Wind. See *Close-Hauled*.

Open Boat. A boat with no deck and with a large cockpit.

Outboard. 1) *Athwartships* toward the rail. 2) Outside of but attached to the *hull*. 3) Abbreviation for "outboard engine."

Outhaul. A line that adjusts the position of the clew and foot tension on a boomed sail.

Outpoint. To point higher than another boat.

Outsail. To sail faster than another boat.

Overall Length. See *LOA*.

Overboard. In the water outside the boat.

Overcanvassed. With too much sail set. Also "overpowered."

Overhang. The amount that the bow and stern extend beyond the waterline, measured by subtracting the load waterline length (*LWL*) from the length overall (*LOA*). Illustration on page 109.

Overhaul. 1) To overtake another boat. 2) To check that a boat or piece of gear is ready to use.

Overlapped. The relationship between two boats when part of one boat lies forward of a line projected abeam from the other's aftermost point; or between a jib and a mainsail if, when trimmed tightly, the jib's clew is abaft the mainmast.

Overpowered. See *Overcanvassed*.

Overstand. To fetch a buoy with room to spare.

Overtake. To catch a boat from astern.

Overtrim. To trim too far.

P

Padeye. A metal half-loop secured to a pad bolted to the deck or to a spar. It holds shackles or blocks.

Painter. A short tow or mooring line, one end of which is secured to a dinghy's bow.

Panel. 1) A strip of cloth used to make a sail. 2) A section of a *shroud* or *mast* between the *masthead*, *spreaders*, and *deck*. 3) The area where the master electrical switches, read-outs for electronic devices, or controls for *hydraulic adjustors* are located.

Panting. Severe vibration in a hull caused by waves and the boat's motion. Also, "oilcanning."

Parallel Rulers. Two small wooden or plastic strips linked and held parallel by arms, and used to transfer bearings and courses to and from the compass rose on a chart. See *Compass Rose.*

Part. 1) To break. 2) A section of the fall, or *line* between two blocks in a *tackle*.

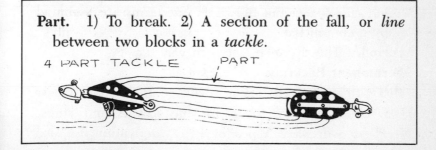

4 PART TACKLE   PART

Partners. The opening in the deck through which the mast passes.

Parts of the Boat. The *hull*, *rigging*, *sails*, *spars*, and their components.

Passage. A non-stop sailing trip lasting longer than two days.

Passageway. A corridor between *cabins*.

Pawl. A hinged pin in a *winch* that, when engaged between teeth, locks the winch and keeps it from backing off (turning counterclockwise).

Pay Off. See *Head Off*.

Pay Out. To ease, to unreel, a line.

Pedestal Steering. A boat's steering system featuring a wheel on a pedestal in the cockpit.

Pelican Hook. A hinged hook with a retaining link. It is usually used to permit opening a section of a life line.

Pelorus. A device used to take a relative *bearing*.

Pendant. A short length of wire or line used for a specialized purpose. A "jib tack pendant" between the tack and deck raises the jib above waves. A "mooring pendant" is used to secure the boat to the mooring. Pronounced "pennant."

Performance Cruiser. A fast *cruiser* or *cruiser-racer*.

Performance Handicap Racing Fleet (PHRF). A *rating rule* for racing in which handicaps are assigned by a committee.

Period. The distance between waves.

Permanent Backstay. See *Stay*.

PFD. Personal flotation device, the U.S. Coast Guard's pre-1988 term for life jackets and rings. There were five types of PFD, depending on use and buoyancy: I (now called Off-Shore Life Jacket); II (Near-Shore Life Vest); III (Flotation Aid); IV (Throwable Device); V (Special Purpose Device).

Phase Characteristics. See *Characteristrics.*

Pier. A narrow platform, generally on posts, built out into the water and providing access from the shore to boats.

Piling. A post supporting a *pier* or *float.*

Pilot. 1) A qualified, usually licensed seaman who guides ships into and out of ports. 2) To steer or set a boat's course into or out of a harbor or alongshore.

Pilotage. The art and science of *piloting.*

Pilot Books. Government publications listing location and characteristics of aids to navigation and other piloting information.

Pilot Charts. Publications showing probable weather conditions and current patterns. There is one chart for each month.

Pilot House. A *cabin* on *deck,* usually just *forward* of the *cockpit.*

Piloting. *Navigation* within sight of land, as compared with *celestial navigation* and offshore navigation with electronics. Also, "coastal navigation."

Pin. 1) Slang for *mark.* 2) A metal object that secures rigging. See *clevis pin, cotter pin.*

Pinch. To sail too close to the wind.

Pintle. A rod on a rudder that secures the rudder to the transom by fitting into the gudgeon.

Pitch. 1) The angle a propeller blade makes to the water. 2) The rising and falling of the bow and stern in waves.

Pitchpole. A boat's somersault, stern over bow, caused by a large wave from astern.

Pitting. Eating away, or corrosion, of metal.

Plan. A two-dimensional drawing made by a *yacht designer*. The "sail plan" depicts the sails to be used, the "accommodation plan" shows the cabin arrangement, etc. See *Line Drawings*.

Plane. To skim across the surface of the water at a speed greater than the hull speed. A "planing boat" is a dinghy, scow, or light-displacement keel boat. See *Displacement, Displacement Boat*.

Play. 1) To pay constant attention to the trim of a sheet. 2) A loose fit, as of a tiller in a rudder, of a centerboard in a well, etc.

Plot. To compute and chart a boat's course and position.

Plug. 1) A wooden object ready to be shoved into a hole left by a broken *through-hull fitting*. 2) A form used to make the molds that are required in *fiberglass construction*.

Point. To sail effectively close-hauled. "Pointing ability" is a boat's success at sailing an upwind course closer to the wind than other boats.

Points of Sail. Run, reach, and closehauled. Illustration on page 87.

Pole-Out. See *Wing-and-Wing*.

Polypropylene. A synthetic material used to make buoyant *rope* and insulated clothing.

Pooped. Describes a boat over whose stern a large wave has broken.

Poptop. A cabin top that can be raised to provide good headroom below.

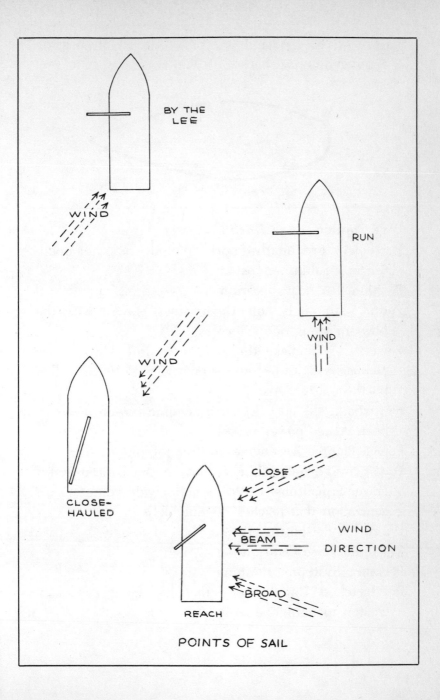

BY THE LEE

WIND

RUN

WIND

WIND

CLOSE-HAULED

CLOSE

BEAM

WIND DIRECTION

BROAD

REACH

POINTS OF SAIL

87

Port.   1) The left-hand side of a boat, facing forward. 2) A commercial harbor. 3) See *Porthole.*

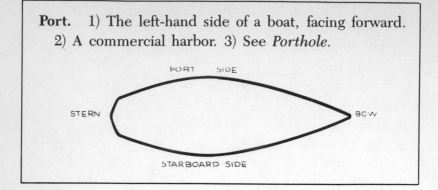

Port Captain.   See *Harbor Master.*

Porthole.   Frequently, "port." Window or other opening in a cabin or topsides.

Position.   A boat's location.

Pound.   To pitch violently in steep waves, with the bow smashing onto the seas.

Power.   1) To make the sails more *full.* Opposite of *Depower.* 2) To be "under power" is to be propelled by the engine. Also "motor."

Powerboat.   A boat driven by engine power; a motorboat. Also, "power vessel."

Power Plant.   An engine and its equipment.

Power Squadron.   Abbreviation for the United States Power Squadrons (USPS), a nationwide volunteer organization that teaches boating skills.

Pram.   A flat-bottomed blunt-bowed dinghy.

Pratique.   See *Quarantine.*

Pressure System.   Running water.

Prestretched Rope.   *Rope* that has been especially treated to minimize stretch.

Preventer. A *line* attached at one end to the *boom* and *running* forward to the *leeward foredeck*. When sailing *downwind*, a strain is taken on the line to "prevent" the boom from swinging across the deck.

Privileged Vessel. See *Stand-On Vessel*.

Production Boat. See *Stock Design*.

Profile Drawing. A plan of the boat from alongside. See *Line Drawings*.

Propeller. Abbreviated "prop" and often nicknamed "screw." Three types of propellers are found on *auxiliary* sailboats. A "solid propeller" has two or three fixed blades. A "folding propeller" has two blades that fold up into a tubular shape when the engine is out of gear in order to reduce water resistance. And a "feathering propeller" has two blades that automatically turn their edges toward the water flow when the engine is out of gear, thereby cutting resistance.

Protest. See *Racing Rules*.

Puff. A short gust of wind. Sometimes, "puffer."

Pulling Boat. Rowboat.

Pulpit. A stainless-steel guardrail around the bow and the stern. "Pushpit" is sometimes used to mean "stern pulpit." Illustrations on pages 8, 111.

Pump. 1) A hand- or motor-driven device that transfers water or fuel. 2) To trim and ease a sail repeatedly to speed up a boat.

Pumping-Out Station. A shore facility where a boat's sewage holding tanks can be emptied and cleaned.

Purchase. See *Tackle*.

Pushpit. See *Pulpit*.

Q

Quadrant. 1) A metal device by which a steering wheel turns the *rudder*. 2) One of the four 90-degree sections of the *compass*, for example "Northeast quadrant" "Southwest quadrant."

Quarantine. Restrictions on a newly arrived crew's activities in a port. The yellow "Q" code flag, flown from the starboard rigging, is a request for clearance ("pratique") by local health officials.

Quarter. The areas on either side between amidships and the stern. A "quartering" sea or wind is from directly toward the quarter (about 45 degrees abaft the beam).

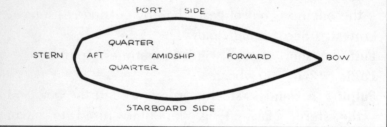

R

Race. 1) A contest or competition between two or more boats. 2) A strong or rapid tidal current.

Race Committee. The group of officials who run a sailboat race.

Racer. A boat designed primarily for racing.

Racer-Cruiser.   A boat whose primary purpose is racing but that is also comfortable enough for cruising. Also "dual purpose yacht." See *Cruiser-Racer*.

Racing Rules.   Rules written by the *International Yacht Racing Union* to keep racing boats from colliding and from unfairly winning races. A *crew* who feels that another boat has violated the rules "protests" the other crew to a "jury" of "judges," who hold a hearing to decide on the merits of the case. See *Foul*.

Radar Reflector.   A metal device hoisted in a boat's rigging that can be picked up on the radar screen of another boat.

Radial Clew, Radial Head.   Describes a sail that has reinforcing *panels* extending finger-like from the corners toward the middle.

Radiotelephone.   A transmitter and receiver linking a boat with the shore, usually over a VHF/FM system.

Rail.   The outer edge of the *deck*. If it is raised, it is a *gunwale* (pronounced "gun'l"). See *Grab Rail (Strap)*.

Raise.   1) To come in view of, to sight an object. 2) To hoist.

Raised Decked.   See *Flush-Decked*.

Rake.   The angle a mast, transom, or bow makes with the perpendicular.

Range.   1) A pair of objects (often *aids to navigation*) that when lined up indicate a safe *course*. 2) To frequent, for example "ranging the Maine Coast." 3) "Tidal range" is the difference in water level between low and high *tides*. 4) "Visibility range" is the distance from which objects can be seen. 5) "Range of positive stability" is the angle of heel at which a boat loses all *stability* and *capsizes*. For example, a boat with a range of 120 degrees will come back upright at any heel angle up to 120 degrees. After that, she will turn over.

Ratchet Block.   A block with a toothed mechanism that permits the sheave to turn in only one way and so snubs a line.

Rating Rule.   A handicapping system for racing boats of different sizes, usually ocean (offshore) racing boats. It produces "ratings," or numerical estimates of boats' potential speed, which in conjunction with time allowances produce handicaps. There are two types of rating rules. A "measurement rule" (like the International Measurement System and the International Offshore Rule) assigns ratings based on the boats' dimensions. A "handicap rule" (such as the Performance Handicap Racing Fleet) assigns ratings based on a committee's evaluation.

RDF.   Radio Direction Finder. A radio receiver that homes on transmitters or beacons. Compass bearings so determined are used in navigating.

Reach.   1) A course across the wind: on a "beam reach" the course is ninety degrees from the true wind direction; on a "close reach" the wind is forward of ninety degrees; on a "broad reach" it is aft of ninety degrees. Illustration on page 87. 2) A narrow body of water between an island and the mainland.

Reacher.   A spinnaker or light-weight jib used when reaching.

Reaching Strut.   A short spar, one end of which is hooked to the mast, that holds the spinnaker after-guy away from the shrouds on a beam or close reach. This decreases stretch in the guy and compression on the spinnaker pole. "Jockey pole" in Britain. Illustration on page 111.

Ready About.   Oral warning to prepare for a tack. It is followed by "hard alee."

Red Sector.   See *Danger Sector*.

Reef.   1) To decrease a sail's area by "reefing" or "taking in a reef." In "roller reefing," the sail is either rolled around a wire at its luff or lowered a few feet

A REEFED BOAT

and rolled around the boom. In "jiffy," "slab," or "tied-in" reefing, the mainsail or mizzen is lowered a few feet, a strain is taken on the bottom of the sail with earings (also called "reefing lines") along the luff and leech, and the excess sail is secured to the foot with light lines called "reef points." Jibs may be jiffy-reefed without earings. A "flattening reef" in a mainsail is a very small reef taken only at the leech in order in flatten the bottom part of the sail. 2) A barely submerged chain of rocks.

Reeve.   To pass one end of a line through a block or eye.

Regatta.   A race or series of races in which a large number of boats participate.

Relief.   Replacement.

Render.   For a line to run freely, with no binding, through a block.

Reverse.   Opposite to normal: a "reverse transom" slopes forward toward the deck; a "reverse sheer" is convex.

Rhumb Line.   The straight-line compass course between two points.

Rib.   See *Frame*.

Ride.   1) To sail, skim, or be driven lightly over the water. 2) To lie or to rest, as "ride at anchor."

Riding Light.   A steady white light on the masthead or hung off the headstay to indicate that a boat is anchored at night.

Rig.   1) To prepare a boat or a piece of gear for use, for example "rig the spinnaker." 2) See *Rigging*.

Rigging.   The *parts of the boat* that control the sails. "Running rigging" includes *halyards, sheets,* and their *blocks* and *fittings.* "Standing rigging" includes *spars, stays,* and their fittings. Also, "rig."

Rigging Screw.   British for *turnbuckle.*

Right.   To bring back upright after a *capsize.*

Right of Way.   The legal right to hold *course* under the *rules of the road.* The boat that does not have the right of way must alter *course.* The "right of way boat" may (or must) stay on course. See *Course, Stand-On Vessel.*

Riprap.   Piles of stone that protect a lighthouse or pier from erosion.

Roach.   The extension of a sail's leech or foot beyond the straight lines from clew to head or clew to tack.

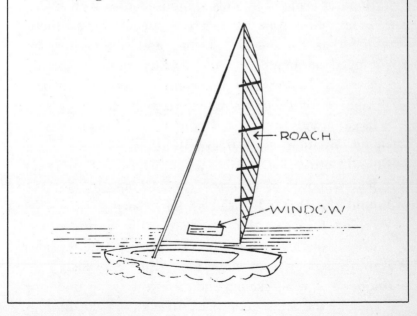

Rod Rigging. *Stays* made of steel rod, which stretches less than *wire rope.*

Rode. See *Anchor Rode.*

Roll. The rhythmic heel of a boat, first to one side, then to the other. In a "roll tack" a racing dinghy is permitted to heel to the old windward side as she comes through the eye of the wind, and is then flattened after her sails fill on the new tack, thus speeding up the tack.

Roller Furler. A device that allows a sail to be rolled up rather than *dowsed* when not in use. A roller furler may also be used to *reef* a sail.

Roller Reef. See *Reef.*

Root In. To dig in.

Rope. Cordage that when cut up for use on a boat is called *line.* The only rope on a boat is the *bolt rope.* Rope is made of strands composed of woven fibers. Today, most rope fibers are made of the synthetic materials *Dacron* and *nylon,* and strands are arranged in "braid" or "laid" construction. In "braid," the strands are woven in a complex network. In "laid rope" (also called "stranded rope"), three or four large strands are twisted around each other.

Rough Weather. See *Heavy Weather.*

Round-Bottom. Describes a boat whose bottom is not flat. Opposite of *V-Bottom.* See *Chine.*

Round Up (Off). To head up (off) sharply.

Rubbing Strake. A fore-and-aft running protrusion, usually just below the rail, that protects the topsides from piers or boats alongside. Also, "rubwale."

Rudder. A wing-like appendage in the water under or behind the after underbody that steers the boat in response to movements by the tiller or steering wheel. A rudder under the hull is called an "inboard rudder." It pivots on a vertical or near-vertical post called the "rudder stock" (also "rudder post") that is built into the rudder's forward edge and that goes up into the hull. Inboard rudders may be "skeg-mounted" or "keel-mounted" (hanging off the trailing edge of the skeg or keel under the boat) or they may be "separate" (independent of the keel). A separate rudder is sometimes called a "spade rudder" in honor of its appearance. A spade rudder that projects forward of the stock is called a "balanced rudder." An "outboard" or "transom-mounted rudder" hangs off the stern. An outboard rudder on a small boat pivots on gudgeons and pintles and usually is removed after sailing. See *Aspect Ratio*.

Rules of the Road.   Official regulations that prescribe how boats should behave in collision situations. There are two nearly identical sets of rules: the 1980 U.S. Inland Navigational Rules (known as the "Inland Rules of the Road"), which govern near *shore*; and the 1972 International Regulations for Preventing Collisions at Sea (known as "COLREGS"), which govern outside demarcation lines shown on charts.

Run.   1) Sailing with the wind *astern*. 2) To *lead* or direct a *line*, for example "run the jib *sheet forward* through that *block*." 3) The boat's *after underbody*. 4) A sailing trip lasting no longer than one day.

Run Before It. To sail on a *run* in *heavy weather*.
Running Backstay. See *Stay*.
Running Lights. See *Navigation Lights*.
Running Rigging. See *Rigging*.

S

Safe Leeward Position. The position of a close-hauled boat when another close-hauled boat on the same tack is just off her windward quarter. The leeward boat then directs the wind to the other boat's disadvantage.

Safety at Sea. The branch of *seamanship* concerned with saving lives and eliminating emergencies afloat.

Safety Harness. For use when footing is unsteady, a chest harness with a tether line that is hooked to the boat or the *jackline*.

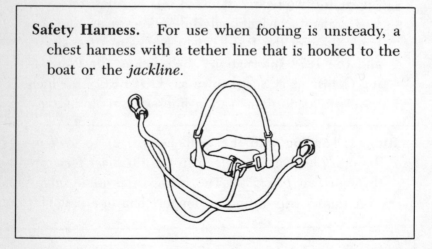

Safety of Life at Sea Conference (SOLAS). A 1983

international conference that established standards for emergency equipment.

Sag. 1) To "sag off to leeward" is to make excessive leeway, to slide to leeward. 2) When the jib is full, the amount the headstay curves to leeward.

Sail. A sailboat's primary means of propulsion. Pronounced as spelled when used alone, but pronounced "sul" when used as a suffix, as in "mainsail." "Working sails" are the mainsail and a small jib. "Light sails" are the spinnaker and other lightweight sails set on a run or reach. "Storm sails," set in heavy weather and stronger winds, are a very small mainsail and jib called the "storm trysail" and "storm jib." A "sail bag" is a sausage-shaped or sack-type bag for stowing sails. "Sail handling" is the art of setting, trimming, and dowsing sails properly. The "sail inventory" consists of the sails onboard.

Sail Area (SA). The square footage of the *sail plan*.

Sail-Area/Displacement Ratio. A number that determines a boat's *sail area* relative to her *displacement*, or weight, in order to indicate how much driving force she has relative to her weight. The formula has three steps. First, determine the boat's displacement in cubic feet by dividing the total weight by 64 (if the boat is in salt water) or 62.2 (in fresh water). Second, calculate that number to the two-thirds function (square it and then find the cube root). Third, divide the result into the sail area. If the final result is lower than fourteen, the boat is a heavy, underpowered *cruiser*. If it is between fourteen and sixteen, she is a normal *cruiser-racer*. If it is above sixteen, she probably is a *racer*. See *Displacement/Length Ratio*.

Sailboard. A fast, maneuverable boat that looks like a surfboard with a sail. The Windsurfer (a trademark) was one of the first sailboards. Abbreviated "board." To sail a sailboard is to go "boardsailing" or "windsurfing." A sailor on a sailboard is a "boardsailor."

Sailcloth. Fabric used to make sails. See *Dacron, Kevlar, Mylar, Nylon*.

Sail Control. A line used to *trim* the sail and adjust its shape. See *Cunningham, Outhaul, Sheet, Traveler*.

Sail Cover. Canvas or synthetic cloth tied over a furled sail to protect it from dirt, wind, weather, and sun.

Sail Handling. Hoisting, trimming, and lowering of sails.

Sail Hank. See *Hank*.

Sailing Trim. See *Trim*.

Sailmaker. A sail designer and manufacturer.

Sail Needle. A sturdy and sharp triangular needle used to sew and mend sails or rope.

Sailor. A person who can handle a sailboat knowledgeably.

Sail Shape. See *Chamber, Sail Control, Trim*.

Sail Slide, Sail Slug. A metal or plastic device secured to the luff of a mainsail or mizzen and installed over a track or in a groove on the back of the mast.

Sail Stop. A narrow length of sturdy fabric used to tie a *furled* sail to a *boom* or *deck*. Also "gasket," "sail tie."

Sail Tie. See *Sail Stop*.

Sail Trim. See *Trim*.

Salon. See *Saloon*.

Saloon. The main cabin, if it has no berths. Frequently, and mistakenly, "salon" or "lounge."

Samson Post. See *Bitt*.

Sandwich Construction. See *Fiberglass Construction*.

Sand Yacht. A sailboat that rides on wheels over sand and other land surfaces instead of on water.

Satellite Navigation (SATNAV, NAVSAT). A system of navigation in which signals from satellites are interpreted by an onboard receiver/computer. The Global Positioning System (GPS) is a satellite navigation system using more than a dozen satellites.

Scale. See *Chart*.

Scantlings. The construction specifications: dimensions (e.g., of strake, frame, or other part) or nature of material to be used (e.g., type of fiberglass cloth).

School Ship. A vessel used in the training of young seamen.

Schooner. A multimasted boat in which the most forward mast ("foremast") is shorter than those aft.

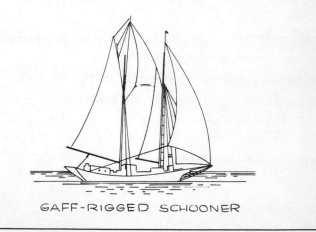

GAFF-RIGGED SCHOONER

Scope. When anchoring, the ratio between the amount of *anchor rode* let out (subtracting the boat's freeboard) and the water's *depth*.

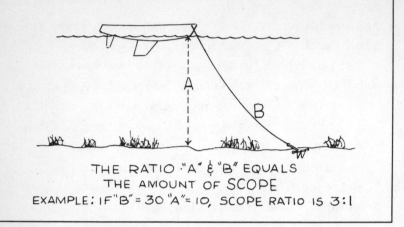

THE RATIO "A" & "B" EQUALS
THE AMOUNT OF SCOPE
EXAMPLE: IF "B"= 30 "A"= 10, SCOPE RATIO IS 3:1

Scow. A fast flat-bottomed blunt-bowed type of racing boat, from sixteen to thirty-eight feet *LOA*; it is popular on small lakes.

Scratch Boat. In a handicap race, the boat with the highest rating.

Screw. See *Propeller*.

Scud. 1) To run before a strong wind or gale. 2) Ragged broken clouds.

Scull. To row a boat with a single oar worked over the stern.

Scuppers. Drains on deck or in the cockpit.

Sea. 1) A large body of salt water, smaller than and often feeding into an ocean, sometimes landlocked. 2) A large wave. 3) "To go to sea": sail offshore. 4) "At sea": in a boat offshore.

Sea Anchor. A parachute-shaped, fabric object dragged *overboard* from the *bow* in *heavy weather* to keep the bow pointed into the waves. Compare with *Drogue*.

Seabag. A cylindrical canvas or synthetic fabric bag for clothes and gear; practical for the sailor because it takes little room when empty.

Sea Boots. Rubber boots worn with non-skid soles.

Sea Breeze. An onshore breeze—i.e., a wind whose direction is toward the shore.

Sea Cock. A valve that opens and closes a through-hull fitting. It prevents water from backing up into the boat.

Sea Conditons. The size and interval of waves.

Seafarer. A person at home in a boat at *sea*.

Seagoing. Describes a boat or person capable of going to *sea*.

Seakindly. Describes a boat that is relatively comfortable in *heavy weather*. See *Forgiving*.

Seam. 1) On a hull, where metal plates or wooden planks meet. 2) On a sail, where panels are sewn together, sometimes tapered from luff to leech to give it shape.

Seaman, Seawoman. An especially knowledgeble sailor.

Seamanship. The art and science of sailing a boat competently, safely, comfortably, and enjoyably in all conditions.

Search and Rescue Mission (SAR). A search for distressed vessels by the U.S. Coast Guard or some other agency.

Sea Room. Navigable water sufficient for safe maneuvering, considering the conditions.

Seaway. Sea conditions marked by relatively steep waves.

Seaworthy. Describes a boat that will survive rough weather. See *Forgiving*.

Section. Cross-section of a hull, as shown in the plans. See *Line Drawings*, *Midships Section*.

Sector. The arc in which a lighthouse light is visible. See *Danger Sector*.

Secure. To tie down or fasten.

Seize. To secure one line to another or to a fitting with small light line.

Self-Bailing. Describes a cockpit that is automatically emptied of water because it is above the waterline and gravity pulls the water through scuppers.

Self-Steerer. A device that helps the boat steer herself without the need of electricity. Compare with *Automatic Pilot*.

Self-Tacking Jib. A jib whose sheet is led to an athwartships running traveler so that, like the mainsail, the jib can be tacked or jibed without having to change sheets.

Self-Tailing Winch, Self-Tailer. See *Winch*.

Separate Rudder. See *Rudder*.

Serving. *Light line* wound around a wire splice to protect against corrosion and chafe.

Set. 1) To raise a sail. 2) The *compass direction* toward which the *current* is flowing. See *Drift*.

Settee. A bench in a cabin that can be easily converted into a berth.

720 Rule. See *360/720 Rule*.

Sextant. A device used to measure the altitudes of heavenly bodies. Using tables, the navigator can determine the boat's position. Sometimes, "yoke."

Shackle. A metal hook or loop that is fastened with either a clevis pin, a screw pin ("screwshackle"), or a spring-loaded lock pin ("snapshackle"). It is used to secure a line to a fitting or a sail or one fitting to another.

Shakedown Cruise. The first (familiarization) sail in a new boat.

Shake Out a Reef. To untie or unroll one reef. See *Reef*.

She. The pronoun usually used when referring to an individual pleasure boat. "It" is generally used when referring to a design, a *class*, or a commercial or naval vessel.

Sheave. See *Block*.

Sheer. 1) The curve of the *rail*, or outer edge of the *deck*, from *bow* to *stern*. With "reverse sheer" the curve is convex. With "flat" or "straight sheer," there is no curve at all. 2) To turn violently when at anchor.

Sheet. A line used to adjust the shape and angle of attack of a sail. The "main sheet" is used on the mainsail, the "jib sheet" on the jib, the "spinnaker sheet" on the spinnaker, etc. To "sheet in" is to pull on a sheet.

Sheet Stopper. See *Lock-Off*.

Shell. The outside frame of a block. The sides are "cheeks."

Shellback. An old sailor.

Shift. To change direction, for example "wind shift," "current shift."

Shifty. Describes a wind constantly changing in direction.

Ship. 1) The largest type of vessel, either a square-rigged or power vessel. 2) To put something where it belongs. 3) To go aboard—a "shipped wave" has come aboard.

Shipmate. A fellow crewmember.

Ship's Clock. A clock that tells time with hands as well as with a system of bells that works on a four-hour cycle. "One bell" is 12:30, 4:30, or 8:30; "two bells" is 1, 5, or 9; and so on every half-hour to "eight bells" at 4, 8, or 12.

Ship's Papers. Documents required for inspection under the law, including certificate of enrollment or registry, license, crew and passenger lists, etc.

Shoal. An area of shallow water. "Shoaling water" gradually becomes shallower.

Shoal-Draft. Describes a boat with a draft of less than five feet.

Shock Cord. Elastic rope.

Shoot. 1) To make progress toward an object while luffing into the wind. 2) To measure with a sextant the angle between the horizon and a heavenly body.

Shore. 1) Coastline. 2) A support for a hauled-out boat.

Short-Ended. A boat having short overhangs.

Shorten Down. To reduce sail area.

Shortened Sail. *Reefed* or otherwise sailing with less than the maximum amount of sail in the *sail plan*.

Short-Handed. With a smaller crew than usual.

Short Seas. Waves with a short period.

Shroud. See *Stay*.

Side Deck. The deck on either side of the house.

Side Lights. The red and green running lights.

Silverware. Prizes, trophies.

Single Block. See *Block*.

Single-Bottomed. Describes a boat having no space between the cockpit sole and the bottom. See *Double-Bottomed*.

Singlehanded. With a *crew* of one.

Sister Ships. Boats built to the same design.

Skeg. A narrow, shallow appendage running between the keel and the rudder.

Skipper. The person in charge of a boat's crew while she is under way.

Skippers' Meeeting. A pre-race meeting at which oral instructions are given by the race committee.

Skylight. A window that serves as a hatch cover and admits light below. See *Porthole*.

Slab Reef. See *Reef*

Slack. 1) Not taut (a sheet or stay). 2) To ease (a sheet). 3) Not moving (tidal current).

Slat. See *Companionway*.

Slatting. The motion or sound of sails that are flapping as the boat rolls in a calm.

Sleigh Ride. A fast, exciting run before the wind in fresh air. Originally "New Bedford Sleigh Ride," describing the towing of a whaleboat by a harpooned whale.

Slicker. See *Foul Weather Gear*.

Slip. A ship's berth between two piers.

Sloop. A single-masted sailboat with the mast less than one-third of the LOA abaft the headstay. On a cutter the mast is abaft that point.

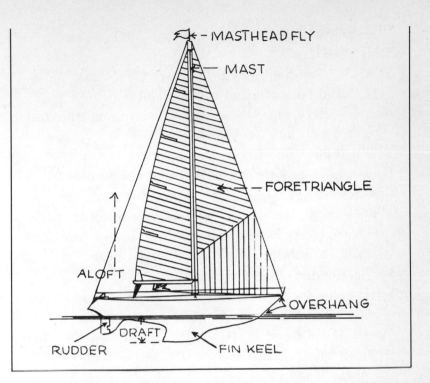

Labels in image: MASTHEAD FLY, MAST, FORETRIANGLE, ALOFT, OVERHANG, DRAFT, RUDDER, FIN KEEL

Slop. Confused seas, with different-sized waves coming from several directions.

Slot. The area between the *luff* of one sail and the *leech* of the sail *forward* of it.

Slug. See *Sail Slide, Sail Slug.*

SMG. See *Speed Made Good.*

Snaphook. A metal hook with a spring-loaded retaining pin. It is used to secure a sail to a stay or a line to a fitting. See *Hank.*

Snapshackle. See *Shackle.*

Snatch Block. See *Block.*

Snub. To take some of the strain off a pulling *line* by wrapping it once around a ballard, horn *cleat* or *winch*, or by leading it through a ratchet block.

Soft.   See *Light*.

SOLAS.   See *Safety of Life at Sea Conference*.

Sole.   The floor of a cabin or cockpit.

Sound.   To measure the depth of water under the boat or fuel in a tank on board.

Sound Buoy.   See *Buoy*.

Soundings.   See *Off Soundings* and *On Soundings*.

Sou'wester.   1) Fresh wind from the southwest; in some areas, "smoky sou'wester" because of the light fog produced by the dampness it brings from the sea. 2) A waterproof hat with a large beak.

Spade Rudder.   See *Rudder*.

Spar.   Generic term for poles that support sails, among them *boom, gaff, mast* and *spinnaker pole*.

Speed Made Good (SMG).   The speed that the boat effectively makes. Also "speed over the bottom." See *Course Made Good*.

Speedometer.   An instrument that measures the boat's speed through the water and shows it on an indicator. Also "knotmeter."

Spindrift.   Sea spray; white mist driven from waves by the wind.

Spinnaker.   A large, lightweight sail set *forward* of the *mast* when sailing *downwind*. Also called "chute," "kite," "spi."

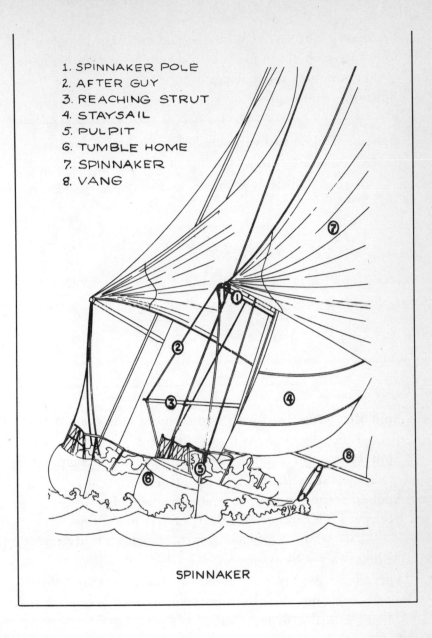

1. SPINNAKER POLE
2. AFTER GUY
3. REACHING STRUT
4. STAYSAIL
5. PULPIT
6. TUMBLE HOME
7. SPINNAKER
8. VANG

SPINNAKER

Spinnaker Net. A web of line and shockcord hung in the foretriangle to prevent the spinnaker from wrapping around the headstay.

Spitfire. Storm jib.

Splice. To join two wires or *lines* or to put an eye in a wire or line by interweaving their strands.

SPLICE DEADENDED ON A BECKET

Split Rig. Any boat with two or more masts: a ketch, yawl, or schooner. Also, "divided rig."

Split Tacks. To take the tack different from a competitor's when racing on an upwind leg or a run.

Spokes. The handles on a steering wheel.

Spray. Flying water. "Light spray" is like a fine rain. "Heavy spray" may severely obstruct visibility and the crew's activity on deck.

Spreader. A strut on the side of the mast that holds out a shroud, thereby increasing its leverage on the mast in order to limit side bend.

Spring Lines. *Docking lines* that help the boat lie

parallel to a *float* or *pier* and control *fore and aft* movement. The "forward spring line" is *cleated* on the boat near the cockpit and runs *forward* to a cleat on the float near the *foredeck*. The "after spring line" is cleated on the foredeck and runs aft to the float longside the cockpit. Abbreviated "spring."

Spring Tide. See *Tide*.

Squall. A sudden local storm. A "wind squall" has more wind than rain, a "rain squall" more rain than wind.

Squirrelly. Unstable, hard to steer in a straight line.

Stability. A boat's resistance to wind and wave. "Directional stability" indicates resistance to forces that throw a boat off *course*. Generally, however, stability refers to resistance to *heeling*. A "stable boat" does not heel very much; an unstable (or "tender") boat tips readily. "Initial stability" is a boat's resistance to heeling at shallow angles of heel. "Ultimate stability" is her resistance at high angles. See *Range* Def. No. 5.

Stanchion. A metal support at the edge of the *deck* that holds up the *lifeline*.

Standing Part. The portion of a *line* that is not moved while a *knot* is being tied. Illustration on page 11.

Standing Rigging. See *Rigging*.

Stand-On Vessel. The boat or ship allowed, and sometimes required, by the *rules of the road* to hold *course* in collision situations. Opposite of *Give-Way Vessel*. Once called "privileged vessel."

Starboard. Facing forward, the right-hand side of a boat. Illustration on page 88.

Start. 1) To ease (sheets). 2) The beginning of a race.

Stateroom. A sleeping cabin on a boat.

Stays. Wires and rods that support the mast either from forward, the side, or aft. The primary forward stay is the "headstay" running from the bow to high up the mast. Some boats have a "forestay" running from the foredeck to part-way up; a "babystay" running from the foredeck to slightly up; and/or "jumper stays" near the hounds. The stays on the side are called "shrouds" or "sidestays": the "upper shrouds" run to the masthead, usually over spreaders, while the "lower shrouds" run part-way up. (See *Discontinuous Shroud, Spreader*.) The after stays are called "backstays." The "permanent backstay" runs from the stern to the masthead. Some boats have "running backstays," which run from the stern or side decks to part-way up the mast to keep the middle of the mast from buckling.

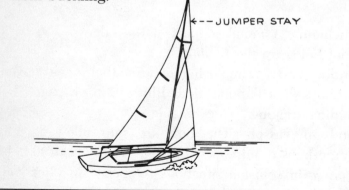

←--JUMPER STAY

Stay Adjustor. A *hydraulic adjustor, turnbuckle,* or *tackle* used to quickly adjust the length of a *stay,* usually the permanent backstay.

Staysail. 1) On a yawl, ketch, or schooner, a sail hung between two masts. 2) Abbreviation for "forestaysail." See *Jib*.

Steadying Sails. Small sails that dampen a boat's roll in waves.

Steerage Way. Enough speed to steer a boat.

Steerer. The person who is steering. Sometimes "helmsman."

Steerer's Errors. Mistakes made by a *steerer* that cause a boat to sail off *course*.

Stem. The forward point of the bow.

Stem Roller. See *Bow Roller*.

Step. To raise the mast, with its butt (bottom) fitted to the *mast step*.

Stern. The back of the boat. The "stern wave" is the wave near the stern that is created by the hull passing through the water.

Stiff. 1) Stable, resistant to heeling (a boat). 2) Fresh (breeze).

Stinkpot. Term of opprobrium for "power boat."

Stock. See *Rudder*.

Stock Design. A plan from which many sister ships are built by the same manufacturer. These boats are sometimes called "stock boats" or "production boats." See *Custom Design, Sister Ships*.

Stop. 1) To tie thread ("stopping twine") or to loop rubber bands around a *spinnaker* before *hoisting* so it does not *fill* prematurely. 2) Abbreviation for *sail stop*.

Stopper. See *Lock-Off*.

Storm Anchor. A heavy, highly reliable anchor used in strong winds.

Storm Sail. See *Sail.*

Stow. To put an object away in its proper place.

Stowage (Storage). A *locker*, bin, or other location in which to *stow* (or "store") objects.

Stranded Rope. See *Rope.*

Strategy. See *Tactics.*

Stream. To let a line run out overboard and astern.

Stretch. The amount of give in a sail or a line under tension before it tears or breaks.

Strike. To lower (a sail or the colors).

Stringer. A reinforcing frame laid fore and aft in the bilge.

Strong Wind. Wind of 22–27 knots.

Stuffing Box. A container built around the propeller shaft where it passes through the hull to prevent the entrance of water.

Sump. The very lowest part of the bilge, where water is most likely to collect.

Surf. To ride down the face of a wave. "Surfing ability" is a boat's readiness to surf.

Survey. To examine a boat closely for structural weakness.

Survival Conditions. Weather so dangerous that the boat may sink or be severely damaged.

Survival Suit. A thick outfit covering the whole body that keeps the wearer warm and afloat for extended periods of time.

Swage. To secure, by rolling under pressure, the end of a wire rope into the cavity of a fitting.

Swell. Long, fairly low waves caused by a distant storm.

Swimming Ladder. A small ladder lowered over the *transom* or *topsides* for swimmers to use when climbing back *aboard*.

T

Tabernacle. A box projecting above the deck into which the mast is stepped. The mast is secured with two pins, one of which can be removed to permit lowering the spar onto deck.

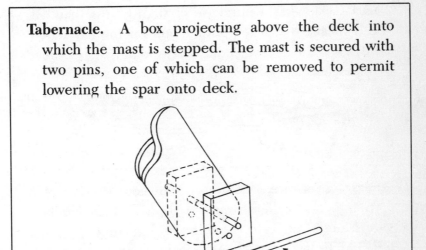

Tabling. Cloth reinforcement on the edge of a sail.

Tack. 1) With "starboard" or "port," describes the side of the boat over which the wind passes. 2) To head up through the eye of the wind and then head off on the other tack; "come about." 3) The lower forward corner of a mainsail or jib; the corner of a spinnaker near the spinnaker pole. Illustration on page 8.

Tack Down.   To secure the tack of a sail.

Tackle.   Pronounced "taykle." A system of *blocks* and *line* that increases hauling power. The pulling end of the line is called the "fall" and the sections between the blocks are called "parts." The number of parts determines the power of the tackle, with every part increasing the "purchase" (power ratio) by a factor of one, less the effect of friction. For example a "four-part tackle" has a purchase of slightly less than 4:1; this means that a ten-pound pull on the fall should lift a weight of just under forty pounds. Also called "block and tackle."

4 PART TACKLE

Tactics.   In a race, decisions about course relative to other boats. Differs from "strategy," which involves decisions relative to the wind and current.

Tail.   1) To haul on a sheet or halyard around a winch being turned by another crewmember. 2) To follow closely, usually before the start of a match race between two boats.

Tall Buoy.   A small mooring buoy with a tall rod that may be easily picked up from the deck of a boat.

Tang.   A metal strap bolted to a mast and to which a stay or halyard block is secured.

Tank Test.   A test of the potential speed of a design; a scale model is pulled through water and the resistance measured.

TD. Abbreviation for "time difference," the basic display on a Loran-C navigation instrument. See *Loran-C*.

Team Race. A race in which two teams, each of three or four boats, race against each other; the winning team has the best total score.

Telltale. A short length or yarn or ribbon that is tied to a *stay* to indicate *apparent wind* direction, or secured to a sail to help *trim* it properly.

Telltale Compass. See *Compass*.

Tender. 1) Unstable, tippy; see *Stability*. 2) A boat specifically assigned to service another boat by delivering supplies and transporting her crew to and from shore.

The. Usually precedes the name of a commercial ship or boat, but not that of a yacht.

Thimble. A metal or plastic round or (usually) heart-shaped loop deeply scored on its outer rim. Worked into an eye splice, it limits chafe on the rope or wire.

360/720 Rule. A provision in the racing rules that allows a boat to avoid disqualification for a foul by taking the alternative penalty of sailing either one (360-degree) or two (720-degree) complete circles.

Three Sheets to the Wind. Drunk.

Through-Fastened. Bolted, not screwed.

Through-Hull Fitting. A drain, intake, or other fitting passing through the skin of the hull. See *Sea Cock*.

Thwart. Seat in a small boat.

'Thwartships. See *Athwartships*.

Tide. The rise and fall of the level of the oceans in phase with the moon's changing gravitational force.

"Spring tides" are especially high and come during the new and full moon; "neap tides" are especially low and come at the quarter moon. Tide is distinguished from current (the horizontal motion of water driven by wind or by the change in tides).

Tide Rip. Rough water caused by fast-moving tidal currents, either over shallow water or in conflict with each other.

Tide Table. A government or privately-published schedule of the rise and fall of the *tide*. A "tidal current table" provides time and speeds of maximum and minumum tidal *currents*.

Tied-In Reef. See *Reef*.

Tight. Taut, straight, for example "tight leech." Opposite of *loose*.

Tiller. A bar that turns the *rudder* to *steer* the boat when there is no steering wheel. A "tiller extension" (also "hiking stick") is a hinged extension that allows the *steerer* to work the tiller from far off to one side, where he or she can see the *jib*.

Time Allowance. The handicap in time allowed a slower boat by a faster one under *rating rules*.

Time Difference (TD). See *Loran-C*.

Toe Rail. A low rail set on deck to provide better footing when the boat is heeled.

Toggle. A U-shaped cast-metal fitting that links a stay's turnbuckle with its chainplate. The toggle permits some horizontal movement so that the turnbuckle is not bent when the stay is pulled out of line.

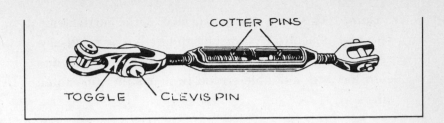

COTTER PINS

TOGGLE   CLEVIS PIN

Ton Classes. See *Level Racing.*

Top Off. To fill fuel or water tanks completely.

Topping Lift. A line or wire from aloft that holds up the spinnaker pole and (on cruising boats) the booms. Illustration on page 53.

Topsides. The side of a hull above the waterline.

Topsiders. See *Deck Shoes.*

Tow. To pull. A boat "under tow" is being pulled.

Track. 1) The summary of a boat's *course made good* over a period of time. A boat that "tracks well" holds her *course* without too much work by the *steerer.* 2) Length of metal on which *jib leads, cars* for *travelers* and *spinnaker poles,* and *sail slides* move.

Trade Winds. Regular and generally strong winds that persist in the equatorial regions. Their predictability made them valuable for commercial sailing ships, hence their name.

Traditional. Term frequently applied to older designs, usually having long keels and low freeboard and long overhangs.

Trailable. Describes a small cruising boat that is narrow, shallow, and light enough to be towed behind a car on a trailer and launched from a ramp.

Transducer. Sensor for a *depth sounder* or *speedometer.*

Transom. The athwartships surface at the furthest aft point of a boat. A "transom stern" has a relatively large transom angled aft; a "reverse transom" is angled forward; a double-ended boat has no transom at all.

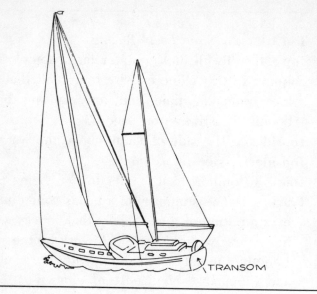

TRANSOM

Transom Ladder. See *Swimming Ladder*.

Transpac. A biennial race from Los Angeles, California, to Honolulu, Hawaii.

Traveler. An *athwartships* running *track* with an adjustable *car* to which the main *sheet* is led. The traveler allows athwartships adjustment of the main *boom*.

Travel Lift. A large device for hoisting boats out of the water and transporting them to their *cradles*.

Trapeze. A wire hanging from the mast which, when attached to a harness, permits a crewmember to stand out from a one-design on the windward rail to improve stability.

Trim. 1) To pull on a sheet. 2) The shape of a sail. 3) The attitude of a boat. "trimmed by the *bow (stern)*" means that the bow (stern) is lower than desired.

Trimaran. A boat with three hulls.

Trim Tab. A flap on the after edges of the keels of some racing boats with separate rudders. Adjusting its angle of attack to the water will make the boat point higher and turn faster.

Trip. To break an anchor loose from the bottom with a "tripping line" attached to the top, or crown.

Trotline. A line between two anchors or between an anchor and the shoreline to which one or more mooring buoys are attached.

Truck. The masthead.

True Direction. The geographical compass direction, shown in the outer ring of a compass rose where the North arrow points to the North Pole. See *Magnetic Direction.* Illustration on page 25.

True Wind. The direction and strength of wind felt on a boat that is not moving. See *Apparent Wind.*

Trunk. The top and sides of the cabins appearing above deck. Also, "house," "deckhouse."

Trysail. See *Sail.*

Tumble Home. The amount the topsides curve inboard toward the deck. Illustration on page 111.

Tune. To adjust running and standing rigging until they are at optimum tension and position. "In tune" describes a boat with her rigging properly tuned.

Turnbuckle. A tension-adjusting device composed of threaded rods joined by a threaded barrel. It is usually found at the bottom of a stay. British: "rigging screw."

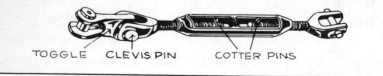

TOGGLE   CLEVIS PIN   COTTER PINS

Turning Block. See *Block.*

Turtle. To turn upside down.

Tweaker. See *Twing.*

Twing. A control line that pulls a spinnaker *sheet* down to prevent the *spinnaker pole* from lifting. Also "tweaker."

Twins. Two jibs of equal size and shape that are set on cruising boats on either side of the headstay when running. With the mainsail lowered, a boat rigged with twins will steer easily.

Twist. The degree to which a sail's leech aims to leeward at increasing heights above the boom.

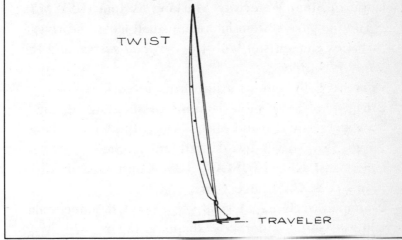

Two Block. To raise a halyard all the way.

U

Unbend. To detach or remove.

Under. Prefix denoting status. A boat "under tow" is being pulled, "under sail" is being sailed, "under power" is being propelled by her engine, "under way" is making *way*.

Under Bare Poles. With no sails hoisted.

Underbody. The hull below the waterline.

Undercanvassed. With too little sail set. Also, "underpowered."

Under Power. With the engine running and in gear.

Underpowered. See *Undercanvassed.*

Unfair. Rough. Opposite of *fair.*

Uniform State Waterway Marking System (USWMS). The *buoyage* system for many small lakes and rivers. It uses elements of both the *cardinal system* and the *lateral system.*

Unreeve. To remove a line from a block.

Unrig. To disassemble running or standing rigging.

Upwind. The direction from which the wind is blowing. Also "to windward" and "to weather."

U.S. Coast Guard (USCG), U.S. Coast Guard Auxiliary (USCGA). See *Coast Guard.*

U-Shaped Section. A relatively rounded semicircular athwartships underbody shape; compare with *Veed Section.* Illustration on page 72.

U.S. Yacht Racing Union (USYRU). The governing body of sailboat racing in the U.S.

V

Vang. A tackle used to keep the boom from lifting on downwind legs. Also, "boom vang," "kicking strap," "kicker," "boom jack." Illustration on page 111.

Variable. Unsteady in direction and force; applied to current or wind.

Variation. The difference in degrees between *True North* and *Magnetic North* in a given area. The variation and its annual change are shown on charts.

V Bunk. Actually two bunks, generally in the forward cabin, whose feet are joined. Often a wedge-shaped cushion is inserted between the bunks' heads to make a full-width double bunk.

Veed Section. Relatively V-shaped athwartships underbody shape; compare with *U-shaped Section*.

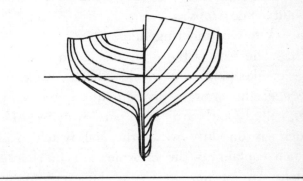

Veer. 1) To ease a line, especially an anchor rode. 2) To shift in a clockwise direction, for example "the wind veered from North to Northeast." Also, "haul." Opposite of *back*.

Ventilator, vent. A device that funnels fresh air below. See *Dorade Ventilator*.

Vessel. Any ship, boat, yacht, or other waterborne craft.

VHF-FM. Very high frequency radiotelephone receiver and transmitter.

Visibility. The clarity with which objects can be seen. See *Range*, Def. No. 4.

Voyage. A passage from home port to a distant port.

W

Wake. The water turbulence that follows a moving boat.

Wandering. Describes a boat with poor directional stability. See *Stability*.

Warp. A tow or mooring line.

Watch. The part of the *crew* that is on duty ("standing" or "keeping" the watch). On a voyage or long *passage*, the crew is divided into watches (usually two, called "starboard" and "port" watches). The "on watch" is on duty while the "off watch" rests. A "watch captain" is the crewmember in charge of a watch. An "*anchor* watch" is the crew on *deck* to keep a *lookout* when the boat is anchored. To "dog the watch" is to follow an irregular watchkeeping schedule for a short while so that the watches do not stand the same hours each day and night. The "mid watch" comes between midnight and dawn.

Waterline. Where the water surface touches the *hull*. "Waterline length" (LWL) is the length of the waterline when the boat is at rest.

Waterlogged. Saturated with water, hence having no buoyancy.

Watermaker. Device that converts salt water into fresh.

Watertight Compartment. A cabin that can be sealed from flooding water by specially constructed doors or hatches.

Waterway. A river, creek, or small lake.

Wave. Generic term for any undulations on the water surface. Very small waves are "ripples"; large ones are "seas." See *Slop* and *Chop.*

Way. A boat's movement through the water. See *Steerage Way.*

Ways. At a shipyard, a marine railway on which a boat is hauled out of the water.

Weather. 1) A storm. 2) To survive (a storm). 3) Windward, upwind. 4) (General) atmospheric conditions.

Weather Cloth. Canvas or synthetic cloth strips tied into the lifelines of a cruising boat to provide the crew with protection from waves.

Weatherfax. An electronic device that prints weather maps from data transmitted over radio frequencies.

Weather Helm. See *Helm.*

Weigh. To raise an anchor.

Wet Locker. *Stowage* area for wet *foul-weather gear* and other damp clothing.

Wet Storage. Keeping a boat in the water, rather than on shore, during the winter.

Wetsuit. A tight-fitting rubber or foam body covering

that conserves body heat in cold air and water. It also provides some buoyancy.

Wetted Surface.   The surface area, in square feet, of a boat's underbody and appendages.

Whip.   1) A single block with a line rove through it, providing 2-to-1 purchase. 2) To secure the strands at the end of a line using light cord called "whipping twine."

Whisker Pole.   A small-diameter spar attached to the mast and the jib's clew when running wing-and-wing.

Whistle Buoy.   See *Buoy*.

Whitbread Race.   A quadrennial around-the-world race for boats with crews.

Williwaw.   A violent gust of wind down a hillside.

Winch.   Mechanical device that increases power while pulling on *halyards*, *sheets*, and other *lines* that are under load. The "winch handle" turns a drum (which usually is geared). Winches have one, two, or three gear ratios. A "self-tailing winch" (also "self-tailer") has a device that *secures* the line as it is winched in.

Wind.   1) Air in horizontal motion, caused by differences in surface temperature or barometric pressure (also, "air," "breeze"). 2) "Wind shift": a change in the wind's direction.

Windage.   Surface exposed to the wind.

Wind Direction.   The *compass direction* from which the wind is blowing.

Windlass.   A winch, powered by hand or motor, for hauling anchors.

Window.   A clear plastic section in a mainsail or jib

that permits the crew to see to leeward from the windward side. Illustration on page 95.

Windsail. A cloth air scoop that catches wind and passes it through a hatch to provide ventilation below.

Windseeker. See *Drifter.*

Wind Sheer. Differences in wind velocity and direction from the *deck* to the *masthead.*

Windsurfer, Windsurfing. See *Sailboard.*

Windward. Upwind, weather. See *Leeward.*

Wing-and-Wing. Sailing on a run with two sails set, one on either side. When a jib is "wung out," its clew usually is held out by a spinnaker pole or whisker pole.

Wire. Slang for *Trapeze.*

Wire Rope. Stainless-steel or galvanized wire filaments twisted to form ropelike lengths with less stretch than rope.

Wishbone Boom. A two-part *boom* that encloses the sail between its two arms rather than hanging off the sail's *foot.* This type of boom is used on *sailboards.*

Working Sails. See *Sail.*

Wung Out. See *Wing-and-Wing.*

Y

Yacht. A well-designed and well-built boat of any size that is used for pleasure.

Yacht Broker.   A salesman who specializes in used and new yachts.

Yacht Club (YC).   A private organization of sailors.

Yacht Designer.   A naval architect who specializes in designing yachts.

Yachtsman, Yachtswoman.   A person who sails for pleasure.

Yard.   See *Boat Yard*.

Yaw.   To swing off *course*.

Yawl.   A two-masted boat; its after mast is smaller than its forward mast and is located abaft the rudder post.